# THE LUMINOUS PROSPERITY GUIDE TO EMOTIONAL INTELLIGENCE

Ammanuel Santa Anna

www.luminousprosperity.com

Copyright © 2024 Ammanuel Santa Anna

All rights reserved

The characters and events portrayed in this book are fictitious. Any similarity to real persons, living or dead, is coincidental and not intended by the author.

No part of this book may be reproduced, or stored in a retrieval system, or transmitted in any form or by any means, electronic, mechanical, photocopying, recording, or otherwise, without express written permission of the publisher.

*"Divitiae in Servitio Lucis"*

WEALTH IN SERVICE OF LIGHT

# CONTENTS

Title Page
Copyright
Epigraph
Introduction ................................................................ 3
Chapter 1: Emotional Intelligence 101: Key Components Explained ................................................................ 5
Chapter 2: Emotional Intelligence: The Key to Understanding and Regulating Your Emotions ................................................................ 12
Chapter 3: Emotional Intelligence: The Key to Personal Success and Wealth ................................................................ 15
Chapter 4: Empathy: The Heart of Emotional Intelligence in Relationships ................................................................ 27
Chapter 5: Empathy: The Heart of Emotional Intelligence in Relationships ................................................................ 34
Chapter 6: Boosting Emotional Intelligence for Fulfilling Relationships ................................................................ 41
Chapter 7: Navigating the Social Landscape with Emotional Intelligence and Communication ................................................................ 47
Chapter 8: Emotional Intelligence: The Secret Sauce of Effective Leadership ................................................................ 52
Chapter 9: Emotional Intelligence: The Key to Success in Every Sphere of Life ................................................................ 59
Chapter 10: Bridging the Gap: Emotional Intelligence in Artificial Intelligence ................................................................ 66
Chapter 11: The Hidden Link between Emotional Intelligence and Non-Dual Abundance ................................................................ 73
The Future of Emotional Intelligence and Non-Dual Prosperity ................................................................ 80
Acknowledgments ................................................................ 81
About the Author ................................................................ 82
Recommended Reading by Ammanuel Santa Anna ................................................................ 83
1. The Playful Path: Overcoming RSD With Joy and Confidence ................................................................ 84
Format: Paperback, Kindle ................................................................ 85
2. The Alchemy of Prosperity: Unveiling Your Inner Renaissance Through Spiritual Wealth ................................................................ 86
Format: Paperback, Kindle ................................................................ 87
3. The Spiritual Executive: How to Thrive In Every Area of Life ................................................................ 88
Format: Paperback, Kindle ................................................................ 89
4. Twin Flames: The Ultimate Guide ................................................................ 90
Format: Paperback, Kindle ................................................................ 91

5. The Law of Attraction for Financial Freedom: Harnessing Inner Power to Create Wealth  92
Format: Kindle  93

# Preface

Welcome to "The Luminous Prosperity Guide to Emotional Intelligence: The Key to Thriving in Work and Life." This book was born out of a deep-seated frustration with the existing literature on emotional intelligence. Too often, I found these books to be verbose, clunky, and lacking in practical application. They were filled with endless pages of research and theory, but they rarely got to the heart of what emotional intelligence truly is and how it can be effectively applied in our daily lives.

As someone who has spent years navigating the complexities of leadership roles, relationships, and even the emerging field of artificial intelligence, I felt there was a need for a book that distilled the core principles of emotional intelligence into clear, actionable insights. My goal was to create a resource that is not only educational and informative but also engaging and varied enough to keep you turning the pages.

In writing this book, I aimed to cover a wide array of perspectives on emotional intelligence. From its role in effective leadership and fulfilling relationships to its application in the realm of artificial intelligence, this book provides a comprehensive overview that will help you understand emotional intelligence from multiple angles. More importantly, it is designed to help you discover the essence of emotional intelligence within yourself and apply it intuitively in your life.

I believe that emotional intelligence is not just a theoretical concept but a practical skill that can transform your personal and professional life. This book is structured to be a practical guide, filled with real-world examples, strategies, and exercises that you can start using immediately. Whether you are a leader looking to inspire your team, a professional aiming to enhance your career, or someone seeking to improve your personal relationships, this book has something for you.

Thank you for choosing to embark on this journey with me. I hope that "The Luminous Prosperity Definitive Guide to Emotional Intelligence" will not only enlighten you but also empower you to thrive in every aspect of your life.

*Warm regards,*

Ammanuel Santa Anna

# INTRODUCTION

Imagine a world where every interaction you have, whether in the boardroom or at the dinner table, is infused with clarity, empathy, and purpose. A world where you navigate the complexities of human emotions with ease, turning potential conflicts into opportunities for deeper connection and understanding. This is the promise of emotional intelligence, and it is the cornerstone of both personal and professional success.

In today's fast-paced and interconnected world, many of us struggle to manage our emotions effectively. We find ourselves overwhelmed by stress, miscommunications, and the constant pressure to perform. Traditional books on emotional intelligence often fall short, bogged down by verbose explanations and clunky theories that fail to provide practical, actionable insights. They leave readers feeling more confused than empowered, unable to apply the concepts to their daily lives.

This book is different. "The Luminous Prosperity Definitive Guide to Emotional Intelligence" is designed to cut through the noise and deliver the core principles of emotional intelligence in a clear, concise, and engaging manner. Whether you're a leader looking to inspire your team, a professional aiming to enhance your career, or someone seeking to improve your personal relationships, this book provides the tools you need to thrive.

In these pages, you will discover the key components of emotional intelligence—self-awareness, self-regulation, motivation, empathy, and social skills—and how to develop and apply them in various aspects of your life. From effective leadership and fulfilling relationships to navigating the emerging field of artificial intelligence, this book offers a comprehensive overview that will help you understand emotional intelligence from multiple perspectives. More importantly, it will guide you in discovering the essence of emotional intelligence within yourself, enabling you to apply it intuitively and effectively.

I wrote this book because I was frustrated with the existing literature on emotional intelligence. Too many books were filled with endless pages of research and theory, but they rarely got to the heart of what emotional intelligence truly is and how it can be effectively applied in our daily lives. My goal was to create a resource that is not only educational and informative but also engaging and varied enough to keep you turning the pages. With over 24 years of experience in mysticism, energy healing, mindfulness, and psychospiritual integration, combined with over 20 years in business, entrepreneurship, and leadership roles, I bring a unique perspective to the subject. This book is the culmination of my journey and my commitment to helping others unlock their potential through emotional intelligence.

As you embark on this journey, I invite you to open your mind and heart to the transformative power of emotional intelligence. This book is not just a collection of theories; it is a practical guide designed to help you navigate life's emotional complexities with greater ease and competence. By the end of this book, you will have the tools and insights needed to achieve personal and professional mastery with grace and ease.

Welcome to "The Luminous Prosperity Definitive Guide to Emotional Intelligence." Let's begin this journey together and unlock the key to thriving in work and life.

# CHAPTER 1: EMOTIONAL INTELLIGENCE 101: KEY COMPONENTS EXPLAINED

In today's fast-paced and interconnected world, emotional intelligence plays a crucial role in both personal and professional success. Understanding and honing this skill can have a profound impact on our relationships, decision-making, and overall well-being. This chapter will delve into the key components of emotional intelligence, shedding light on what it is and why it matters.

## Understanding Emotional Intelligence: The Basics

Emotional intelligence, often abbreviated as EI, forms the bedrock of our ability to navigate the sea of emotions that each of us and those around us experience daily. At its core, EI involves a sophisticated blend of skills that enable individuals to recognize, comprehend, and adeptly manage emotions in themselves and others. This foundational skill set includes self-awareness, which allows us to observe and understand our own emotional states; self-regulation, which gives us the capacity to modulate and express our emotions in healthy ways; motivation, which propels us towards our goals with a clear emotional purpose; empathy, which enables us to connect with and understand the emotions of others; and social skills, which equip us to manage and nurture relationships effectively.

Developing emotional intelligence begins with an inward journey of recognizing and labeling our own emotions. This may seem simple, but it requires an honest and sometimes challenging exploration of our inner emotional landscape. Recognizing our emotions serves as a preliminary step towards understanding their origin and influence on our behavior and decisions. This self-knowledge is crucial, as it lays the groundwork for the next layers of emotional intelligence.

Once we have a grasp on our own emotions, the focus of EI shifts outward, towards recognizing and interpreting the emotional states of others. This outward focus is where empathy and social skills come into play, allowing for richer, more understanding interpersonal interactions. By learning to read the emotional cues of others, we not only enhance our ability to communicate effectively but also our capacity for compassion and connection.

Simultaneously, emotional intelligence involves the delicate art of self-regulation. This means not only managing our own emotions in response to situations and interactions but also choosing how and when to express them in a way that is constructive and appropriate to the context. This skill is invaluable in maintaining emotional balance and resilience, especially in the face of adversity or stress.

In sum, emotional intelligence is a multifaceted capability that encompasses self-awareness, self-regulation, motivation, empathy, and social proficiency. Its development is a continual process, one that enriches our personal lives while also enhancing our interactions and relationships with others. Through the careful cultivation of EI, we unlock the potential to navigate life's emotional complexities with a greater sense of ease and competence, fostering both personal growth and stronger community bonds.

## The Importance of Emotional Intelligence in Personal Growth

At the heart of personal development lies the profound realm of emotional intelligence (EI). It's the silent engine driving our ability to face life's myriad challenges with poise, nurture connections that enrich our existence, and traverse the complex tapestry of human emotions with awareness and grace. The journey of personal growth is, in essence, an intimate dance with our inner selves—a process deeply intertwined with the mastery of EI.

Cultivating emotional intelligence is akin to laying a solid foundation upon which the structure of personal evolution can robustly stand. It's about more than just managing our reactions or understanding what we feel. It's the intricate process of diving deep into the ocean of our emotions, learning to swim in its currents, and eventually, guiding those waters in directions that serve our growth and enhance our interactions with the world around us.

Embracing emotional intelligence in personal development allows us to approach obstacles not as insurmountable barriers, but as opportunities for expansion and learning. When we're firmly rooted in the knowledge of our emotional selves, we navigate through life's challenges with a resilience that is both learned and earned. It's the difference between being at the mercy of our emotional storms and standing at the helm, steering through them with deliberate intent.

Moreover, the role of EI in forging meaningful relationships cannot be overstated. The ability to empathize, to genuinely connect with others on an emotional level, is a catalyst for building trust and understanding. These are the building blocks of relationships that not only endure but thrive, offering us support, joy, and companionship. As we grow in our emotional intelligence, so too do our capacities for compassion, kindness, and genuine connection expand, enriching our personal lives and the lives of those around us.

In the context of personal growth, emotional intelligence is the key that unlocks a deeper understanding of who we are and how we relate to the world. It guides us in aligning our actions with our values, in setting and pursuing goals that resonate with our deepest selves, and in living with authenticity and purpose. The pursuit of EI, therefore, is not just an exercise in emotional management—it's a path to living more fully, with a richer understanding of the human experience and a greater capacity for joy, resilience, and connection.

## The Role of Emotional Intelligence in Professional Success

Emotional intelligence transcends the boundaries of personal development and ventures into the realm of professional excellence. In the intricate dance of workplace dynamics, emotional intelligence emerges as a pivotal player, distinguishing outstanding performers from the rest. It's the invisible thread that weaves through every interaction, decision, and leadership opportunity, shaping the fabric of a successful career.

At its heart, emotional intelligence in the professional sphere is about understanding and navigating the emotional landscapes of ourselves and those we work with. It's about the ability to tune into the undercurrents of office dynamics, to sense the unspoken and respond with acuity and tact. This keen perception enables us to lead with empathy, making decisions that are not only intelligent but also deeply human.

Leaders and team members alike who possess high levels of emotional intelligence are adept at managing stress, adapting to change, and navigating conflicts with a level of grace that preserves relationships and fosters a positive workplace culture. They harness their emotions to fuel creativity and innovation, inspiring those around them and driving teams toward shared goals with a cohesive vision.

Moreover, emotional intelligence lays the groundwork for effective communication. It allows professionals to convey their ideas and feedback in a manner that is respectful and resonant, ensuring that messages are not just transmitted but truly understood and embraced. This skill is invaluable in negotiations, presentations, client relations, and virtually every aspect of professional life where clarity and influence are paramount.

In the pursuit of professional success, emotional intelligence also amplifies leadership capabilities. Leaders with high EI are capable of motivating their teams, not through fear or authority, but by connecting on an emotional level, recognizing their team members 'strengths, aspirations, and challenges. They create an environment where feedback is not only given but also received with openness, fostering a culture of continuous improvement and mutual respect.

Navigating the professional landscape with emotional intelligence does not guarantee a path free of obstacles, but it equips individuals with the insight and adaptability to overcome these challenges more effectively. It's about making strategic decisions not solely based on data or analysis but enriched with an understanding of the human element—where fostering relationships, team cohesion, and employee well-being are viewed as critical components of lasting success.

In essence, emotional intelligence in the workplace is not a nice-to-have—it's a must-have. It's the fuel for professional growth, the catalyst for leadership, and the bridge to more meaningful, productive relationships. By cultivating this critical skill, professionals not only enhance their career trajectories but also contribute to a more empathetic, resilient, and dynamic workplace culture.

## Self-Awareness: The Foundation of Emotional Intelligence

Self-awareness sits at the very heart of emotional intelligence. It's the introspective journey that illuminates our emotional world, shedding light on the feelings and motivations that drive our thoughts and actions. This profound self-knowledge is not merely about recognizing our emotions as they surface; it's an ongoing exploration of the depths from which these emotions emerge, the patterns they weave into our behavior, and the influence they exert over our decision-making processes.

In cultivating self-awareness, we embark on a path of understanding that transcends mere acknowledgment. It involves a deliberate and often challenging engagement with our internal experiences. Through this engagement, we become adept at identifying our emotional triggers and the reactions they provoke. Such insight allows for a level of control and direction over our responses, giving us the power to steer our lives with intention and clarity.

The significance of self-awareness extends beyond the personal realm, casting its influence over every interaction we partake in. By understanding our emotional selves, we gain the ability to navigate social dynamics with greater empathy and finesomeness. This not only enriches our personal relationships but also enhances our professional interactions. When we comprehend the roots of our emotions, we position ourselves to communicate more effectively, to lead with conviction, and to foster an environment of mutual respect and understanding.

Additionally, self-awareness acts as a catalyst for growth. It challenges us to confront uncomfortable truths about ourselves, to recognize our limitations, and to celebrate our strengths. This honest appraisal of our character is essential for personal development, propelling us toward goals that resonate with our deepest values and aspirations.

Moreover, self-awareness is instrumental in cultivating resilience. By recognizing our emotional patterns and understanding their impact, we equip ourselves with the tools necessary to navigate adversity with grace. It allows us to encounter stress and setbacks with a composed demeanor, ensuring that we emerge from such experiences with learned wisdom and strengthened character.

In essence, self-awareness is more than just the foundation of emotional intelligence; it's the compass that guides us through the intricate landscape of human emotions. It empowers us to lead lives marked by purpose, authentic relationships, and a profound understanding of the self.

# Self-Regulation: Mastering Emotional Control

Navigating the landscape of our emotions with agility and intention is the essence of self-regulation. It is the skill that enables us to pause before we act, to assess our emotional responses with clarity, and to choose actions that are in alignment with our values and goals. Mastery of this aspect of emotional intelligence ensures that our emotions serve us rather than control us, allowing us to face life's challenges with a balanced and composed demeanor.

Self-regulation is not about suppressing our emotions or denying their power; rather, it is about recognizing our feelings and understanding their origins, then making informed choices about how we express and act upon them. This discerning approach to emotional management requires a deep level of self-awareness, as it is only with a thorough understanding of our emotional triggers and tendencies that we can begin to moderate our responses effectively.

The practice of self-regulation involves several key strategies, including setting clear, achievable goals for our behavior, monitoring our emotional reactions to various situations, and employing techniques to calm ourselves when we detect signs of emotional upheaval. Techniques such as deep breathing, mindfulness meditation, or simply taking a moment to reflect can be invaluable tools in the self-regulator's toolkit, helping to ensure that our actions are guided by thoughtfulness rather than impulsivity.

Moreover, the ability to self-regulate has profound implications for our interactions with others.

By managing our emotions responsibly, we foster an atmosphere of trust and respect, as colleagues, friends, and family members feel assured that we will respond to situations with consideration and poise. This reliability strengthens our relationships and enhances our ability to collaborate effectively, as we are seen as steady and dependable, even in the face of adversity.

In professional settings, self-regulation is a cornerstone of leadership and teamwork. It allows us to handle stress constructively, to approach conflict resolution with a cool head, and to inspire confidence in those we lead. A leader who demonstrates emotional control not only navigates their own responsibilities with greater ease but also encourages a more emotionally intelligent, resilient workplace culture.

Self-regulation, then, is a dynamic and invaluable component of emotional intelligence, equipping us to traverse the complexities of both our inner world and our external interactions with adeptness and integrity. It is through the practice of self-regulation that we truly harness the power of our emotions to enrich our lives and the lives of those around us.

## Motivation: The Inner Drive Powered by Emotional Intelligence

Motivation, intricately woven with the fabric of emotional intelligence, is the internal force that propels us toward our aspirations and goals. It is our emotions, after all, that fuel our drive for achievement, that stir us to action, and that sustain our commitment to our endeavors over time. This emotional drive is a critical aspect of emotional intelligence, enabling us to channel our passions and energies into pursuits that are meaningful and rewarding.

The relationship between motivation and emotional intelligence is symbiotic. As we become more attuned to our emotions through self-awareness, we also uncover insights into what truly motivates us. This understanding allows us to align our goals with our inner values and passions, creating a sense of purpose that ignites our motivation. When we are deeply connected to the 'why' behind our actions, our motivation transforms from a fleeting spark into a lasting flame.

Moreover, emotional intelligence enriches our motivational landscape by equipping us with the resilience to face setbacks and challenges. It is one thing to be motivated when circumstances are favorable, but quite another to sustain that motivation through adversity. Emotional intelligence, with its emphasis on self-regulation and empathy, provides the emotional agility needed to navigate the highs and lows on the path to our goals. We learn to manage disappointment, adjust our strategies, and draw inspiration from the journey itself, rather than being solely fixated on the destination.

Additionally, motivation is deeply influenced by our ability to envision the future. Emotional intelligence sharpens this vision, enabling us to foresee and emotionally connect with the outcomes we desire. This forward-looking perspective not only fuels our motivation but also helps us to identify and commit to the steps necessary to realize our vision.

Empathy, another cornerstone of emotional intelligence, also plays a vital role in motivation, particularly when our goals involve others or have a broader impact. Understanding and resonating with the emotions and needs of those around us can magnify our motivation, driving us to contribute to something larger than ourselves.

In essence, motivation powered by emotional intelligence is not just about achieving personal milestones; it's about embarking on a fulfilling journey that resonates with our deepest values and emotions. It's about pursuing goals with passion, resilience, and a profound connection to the emotional currents that guide our lives.

## Empathy: Connecting with Others through Emotional Intelligence

Empathy, at its core, is the echo of our own emotions found in the experiences of others. It's the bridge that connects disparate souls, allowing us to peer into the emotional windows of those around us and understand their joys, their struggles, and their fears. This profound capability is a pivotal element of emotional intelligence, serving not just as a tool for better interpersonal relations but as a fundamental aspect of human connection and compassion.

Cultivating empathy requires a delicate balance of listening and feeling. It demands that we step outside the confines of our own perspectives, to don the shoes of another, and to walk a mile in their emotional experiences. This journey into the hearts and minds of others is not merely about sympathy or pity. Rather, it's an active engagement with their emotional reality, acknowledging their feelings as valid and important without judgment.

In the realm of emotional intelligence, empathy is the ingredient that transforms mere interactions into meaningful connections. It allows us to communicate in a manner that resonates on a deeply emotional level, forging bonds of trust and mutual respect. These connections, enriched by empathy, are the foundation of strong, supportive relationships that withstand the tests of time and challenge.

Empathy also plays a crucial role in conflict resolution. By understanding the emotional underpinnings of disagreements, we can navigate disputes with sensitivity and insight, seeking solutions that acknowledge and address the needs and feelings of all parties involved. This empathetic approach to conflict fosters an atmosphere of cooperation and reconciliation, paving the way for positive outcomes and strengthened relationships.

In essence, empathy is the soul of emotional intelligence. It compels us to look beyond ourselves, to embrace the diversity of human emotion, and to connect with others in a manner that is both profoundly human and deeply transformative.

## Social Skills: Navigating Social Interactions with Emotional Intelligence

In the tapestry of human connections, social skills act as the vibrant threads that weave individuals together, enabling seamless and meaningful interactions. These skills, deeply rooted in emotional intelligence, encompass our ability to communicate clearly, collaborate with others, and navigate the intricacies of social dynamics with ease. They are the practical application of our emotional understanding, allowing us to engage with the world around us in a way that is both effective and harmonious.

Mastering social skills involves more than just the ability to speak eloquently or listen attentively. It requires an acute sensitivity to the nuances of social cues and the flexibility to adapt our approach according to the context and the emotional states of those involved. This adaptability is powered by a deep foundation in empathy, enabling us to resonate with others' feelings and respond in ways that foster connection and mutual respect.

Effective communication, a cornerstone of social skills, hinges on our capacity to express our thoughts and emotions in a manner that is both authentic and considerate of our audience. It's about finding common ground and building bridges through words and actions that acknowledge and value the perspectives of others. Similarly, collaboration thrives when we leverage our emotional intelligence to create synergies, drawing on diverse strengths and viewpoints to achieve shared goals.

Conflict resolution, too, is an area where social skills shine. Armed with emotional intelligence, we approach disagreements not as battles to be won but as opportunities for growth and understanding. We navigate these challenges with a focus on finding solutions that honor the emotions and needs of all parties, paving the way for resolutions that strengthen rather than erode relationships.

In essence, social skills empower us to move through the world with a grace that enriches our interactions and deepens our connections. They are the embodiment of emotional intelligence in action, key to nurturing relationships that are both rewarding and resilient.

# CHAPTER 2: EMOTIONAL INTELLIGENCE: THE KEY TO UNDERSTANDING AND REGULATING YOUR EMOTIONS

In today's fast-paced and often stressful world, the ability to understand and regulate our emotions is more crucial than ever. Emotional intelligence plays a significant role in our overall well-being, impacting our relationships, decision-making, and even physical health. By delving into the realm of emotional intelligence, we can gain valuable insights into our emotional landscape and develop strategies to navigate the complex terrain of our feelings effectively.

## The Essence of Emotional Intelligence in Daily Life

In our daily existence, the fabric of emotional intelligence weaves itself subtly yet profoundly into the very core of our interactions and self-perception. This intricate skill set, far from being a mere psychological concept, functions as the bedrock upon which we construct and navigate our social worlds. At its heart, emotional intelligence is about the nuanced understanding of our emotional selves and the emotions of those around us, facilitating a kind of social symphony that enriches our communal bonds.

Delving deeper, emotional intelligence informs our capacity to approach life's myriad situations with a balanced mindset. In the throes of a heated debate, it is the calming voice of reason that allows us to step back, assess our emotional state, and respond with clarity and composure. When faced with the joyous, the mundane, or the sorrowful, it guides our reactions, ensuring that we remain empathetic and considerate of the feelings of others.

Moreover, the ripple effects of sharpening these emotional tools extend into the realms of problem-solving and decision-making. With a firm grasp on our emotional responses, we can approach challenges with a level-headedness that fosters innovative thinking and effective solutions. It's the difference between reacting impulsively and responding with intention—a skill that proves invaluable whether we're navigating personal crises or steering through professional quandaries.

Crucially, emotional intelligence acts as a mediator in our relationships, both personal and professional. It is the foundation upon which trust is built and understanding is deepened. Through its lens, we learn not just to communicate, but to connect, transforming surface-level interactions into meaningful exchanges.

In essence, the mastery of emotional intelligence is akin to learning a new language—the language of human emotion. It is a tool for decoding the complex messages our emotions convey, enabling us to engage with the world in a more connected, compassionate, and considered manner.

## Identifying Your Emotional Landscape

Embarking on the journey of emotional intelligence necessitates a deep dive into the contours of our emotional landscape. It's akin to mapping out a previously uncharted territory within ourselves, discovering the diverse emotional states that inhabit our inner world. This exploration is foundational, for it is only by pinpointing our emotions and understanding what sparks them that we can begin to navigate the complexities of our emotional responses with grace and precision.

The task at hand involves cultivating a keen awareness of our feelings at any given moment. This means paying attention not just to the emotions that surge loudly within us, but also to those that whisper quietly in the background. It's about recognizing the subtleties of our emotional reactions, whether they're ignited by external events or stem from our internal dialogues.

To identify our emotional landscape, we engage in an ongoing process of self-observation and reflection. This may involve pausing throughout the day to check in with ourselves, asking questions like, "What am I feeling right now?" or "Why does this particular situation evoke such a strong emotional response?" It's about being curious about our emotions without passing judgment on them, allowing ourselves to feel without immediately seeking to change or dismiss those feelings.

By becoming adept at recognizing our emotions and understanding their triggers, we unlock vital insights into our behavioral patterns and thought processes. This level of self-awareness is the cornerstone upon which we can start to build our capacity for managing our emotions more effectively. It's not about suppressing what we feel but about acknowledging our emotions and learning from them, thus fostering a more nuanced understanding of who we are and how we interact with the world around us. Through this process, we lay the groundwork for enhanced emotional intelligence, paving the way for greater emotional well-being and more meaningful connections with others.

## The Science of Emotions: What Happens Inside Us

Delving into the science of emotions unveils a fascinating interplay between our physiological states and psychological experiences. At the core of our emotional responses is a complex network involving the brain, nervous system, and various hormones, each playing a pivotal role in how we experience and react to the world around us. When we encounter a stimulus, our brain's limbic system—comprising key structures such as the amygdala, hippocampus, and hypothalamus—springs into action. This system is responsible for processing emotions, memory, and arousal, orchestrating a symphony of reactions that define our emotional experiences.

The amygdala, often termed the alarm bell of the brain, evaluates incoming stimuli for potential threats, triggering a fight-or-flight response when necessary. This primal reaction is underpinned by the release of stress hormones like adrenaline and cortisol, preparing our body to either confront or evade perceived dangers. Meanwhile, the hippocampus plays a crucial role in contextualizing these emotions, linking them to past experiences and informing our future reactions.

On the psychological side, our emotions are shaped by a tapestry of thoughts, beliefs, and social conditioning. How we interpret an event can significantly influence the emotions we experience in response. This cognitive appraisal adds layers of complexity to our emotional lives, making our reactions to similar events uniquely personal.

Understanding the science behind emotions offers us a powerful lens through which we can examine our feelings. It reveals that our emotional responses are not mere whims but are deeply rooted in the intricate workings of our bodies and minds. By exploring the biological and psychological foundations of our emotions, we gain invaluable insights into why we feel the way we do, empowering us to navigate our emotional landscapes with greater awareness and control. This knowledge underscores the profound connection between our emotions and our overall well-being, illuminating the path toward mastering the art of emotional regulation.

# CHAPTER 3: EMOTIONAL INTELLIGENCE: THE KEY TO PERSONAL SUCCESS AND WEALTH

In today's interconnected world, emotional intelligence has emerged as a crucial factor in determining personal success and wealth. By honing this invaluable skill set, individuals can navigate through life's challenges with grace and resilience, paving the way for holistic prosperity and abundance. In this ultimate guide, we will delve into the components of emotional intelligence and explore how each aspect contributes to a life filled with positivity and fulfillment.

## Unpacking Self-Awareness: The Foundation of Emotional Intelligence

Self-awareness is the cornerstone upon which the edifice of emotional intelligence is built. It is the introspective journey to understand one's own emotions, triggers, and the subtle ways they influence our thoughts, behaviors, and interactions with others. This heightened level of personal insight acts as a compass, guiding us through life's complexities with a clearer sense of direction and purpose.

Cultivating self-awareness is akin to developing an inner dialogue that is both honest and constructive. It requires us to tune in to our feelings with an open mind and a willing heart, acknowledging our strengths and vulnerabilities without judgment. This process not only fosters a profound understanding of ourselves but also enhances our capacity for empathy and understanding towards others.

In the realm of personal success and wealth, self-awareness serves as the bedrock of effective decision-making and goal-setting. With a lucid grasp of our emotional states, we can better navigate the highs and lows of our personal and professional lives. It enables us to identify what truly motivates us, align our actions with our values, and pursue our ambitions with tenacity and vigor.

Moreover, self-awareness illuminates the patterns and habits that shape our lives. By recognizing the behaviors that serve us well and those that hinder our progress, we have the opportunity to cultivate habits that propel us towards our desired outcomes. This conscious evolution of self is instrumental in transcending limitations and achieving a state of holistic prosperity.

The journey towards heightened self-awareness is both challenging and rewarding. It demands consistent effort, reflection, and the courage to confront uncomfortable truths about ourselves. Yet, it is through this endeavor that we unlock our full potential and lay the groundwork for a life marked by emotional richness, deep connections, and an abundance of success. Engaging in practices such as mindfulness meditation, journaling, and seeking feedback from trusted peers can accelerate this journey, offering new insights and perspectives that enrich our understanding of ourselves and our place in the world.

Embracing self-awareness is not merely an exercise in personal development; it is an act of empowerment. It equips us with the tools to master our emotions, adapt to change, and forge a path of genuine fulfillment and well-being. As we embark on this path, we cultivate not only a deeper connection with ourselves but also a profound appreciation for the intricacies of the human experience, laying the foundation for lasting personal success and wealth.

## Mastering Self-Management: Steering Through Emotional Turbulence

Mastering self-management is akin to being the captain of your ship in the midst of a storm. It's about having the presence of mind and the ability to control your emotional and behavioral responses, particularly when the waters of life become rough and unpredictable. This aspect of emotional intelligence is crucial, as it enables individuals to steer through emotional turbulence with composure, preventing the tempests from derailing their course towards success and fulfillment.

At the heart of self-management lies the skill of emotional regulation. It's the ability to recognize and manage your emotions, ensuring they don't overpower your actions or cloud your judgment. Imagine facing a high-pressure situation at work or a personal conflict. Without effective self-management, one might react impulsively, letting frustration or anger take the wheel. However, by harnessing self-management, you can navigate these situations with thoughtful responses, keeping your long-term goals and relationships intact.

Self-management also encompasses stress management, a skill increasingly important in today's fast-paced world. It involves identifying stressors and adopting strategies to remain calm and focused. Whether it's through deep breathing, exercise, or time management techniques, effective stress management can enhance your productivity and well-being, acting as a buffer against the negative impacts of stress on your mental and physical health.

Moreover, self-management extends to the motivation and discipline required to achieve personal and professional goals. It's the inner drive that propels you to persevere in the face of setbacks and the self-discipline to maintain focus on your objectives, even when distractions abound. By cultivating this aspect of emotional intelligence, you unlock the ability to pursue your aspirations with unwavering dedication, turning obstacles into stepping stones on the path to success.

Self-management is not only about controlling negative emotions but also about fostering positive ones. Cultivating a sense of optimism and gratitude can elevate your mood and outlook, impacting your interactions with others and your ability to seize opportunities. It's about choosing to focus on the silver linings, even in challenging times, thereby maintaining a trajectory toward growth and prosperity.

In essence, mastering self-management is about developing a deep understanding of oneself and exercising control over one's emotional landscape. It's a dynamic process that requires ongoing attention and refinement. By committing to this practice, individuals can navigate life's challenges with grace, making deliberate choices that align with their values and goals, thereby enhancing their capacity for resilience, achievement, and, ultimately, holistic prosperity.

## Cultivating Social Awareness: Empathy as a Tool for Connection

Cultivating social awareness transcends mere observation; it demands an empathetic immersion into the emotional states of others. This component of emotional intelligence is a beacon for navigating social nuances and fostering deep-rooted connections that are the backbone of personal and professional success. Empathy, the cornerstone of social awareness, is not just about understanding others' emotions but about feeling with them. It is the bridge that connects isolated islands of individual experiences, creating a landscape rich with mutual understanding and respect.

In the quest for holistic prosperity, the ability to step into someone else's shoes and view the world from their perspective is invaluable. It enriches our interactions, transforming them from mere transactions to meaningful exchanges. Empathy paves the way for genuine relationships, grounded in trust and mutual respect. It enables us to perceive the unspoken, to hear the silence amidst the noise, offering insights into the needs and desires of those around us.

This intuitive connection goes beyond personal gain, contributing to a culture of cooperation and collaboration. In professional settings, social awareness fueled by empathy can reveal the underlying currents of team dynamics, guiding leaders and employees alike in navigating the complexities of workplace relationships. It fosters an environment where everyone feels understood and valued, leading to increased engagement, creativity, and productivity.

Moreover, empathy acts as a catalyst for social change. It compels us to act with kindness and consideration, to champion the well-being of others, and to strive for a collective good. In a world where conflicts arise from misunderstandings and a lack of empathy, cultivating this skill is more than a personal asset; it is a societal imperative.

Empathy requires patience, practice, and a willingness to listen deeply. It involves being present, both physically and emotionally, and offering our undivided attention to those in our orbit. This practice may challenge us, pushing us to confront our biases and to stretch our emotional capacities. However, the rewards are immeasurable. By fostering empathy, we not only enhance our own lives but also contribute to a more compassionate and connected world. It is in this interconnectedness that we find the true essence of holistic prosperity and abundance.

## Excelling in Relationship Management: The Art of Communication and Conflict Resolution

At the heart of relationship management lies the mastery of two pivotal skills: effective communication and adept conflict resolution. This segment of emotional intelligence is crucial for nurturing and sustaining healthy, robust relationships that contribute to our personal and collective prosperity. In the dance of human interaction, these skills are the steps that lead us through complex rhythms with grace and coordination, avoiding the missteps that lead to discord.

Effective communication is more than the mere exchange of words; it is an art form that requires active listening, empathy, and the clear expression of one's thoughts and feelings. It's about creating a space where dialogue flows freely, ideas are respected, and voices are heard. Imagine a scenario where a misunderstanding arises with a colleague or loved one. Instead of allowing assumptions to fuel the fire, effective communication encourages curiosity and open-ended questions, paving the way for clarity and mutual understanding. It's a proactive approach that not only dispels doubts but also strengthens the bonds of trust and respect that are essential for any successful relationship.

Conflict resolution, on the other hand, demands a keen understanding of the nuances of human emotions and the dynamics at play. It's about identifying the root cause of disagreements and working collaboratively towards a solution that honors the perspectives of all parties involved. This doesn't mean avoiding conflict but rather embracing it as an opportunity for growth and learning. By approaching disagreements with a problem-solving mindset and a commitment to finding common ground, we can transform potential rifts into opportunities for deepening our connections and fostering an environment of cooperation and mutual support.

In mastering these skills, we not only enhance our own life experience but also contribute to a more understanding and cohesive world. Relationships, after all, are the fabric of our social existence, and by weaving them with care, respect, and authenticity, we create a tapestry of interactions that supports our journey towards holistic prosperity. Excelling in relationship management is not just about navigating the challenges but about celebrating the diversity and richness of human connection, leveraging our emotional intelligence to create a legacy of positive and impactful relationships.

# Emotional Intelligence in the Workplace: Beyond the Personal Sphere

The realm of the workplace is a dynamic and often challenging environment, requiring more than just technical skills or intellectual prowess for true success and leadership. Emotional intelligence, with its multifaceted components, stands as a critical, yet sometimes underappreciated, asset in professional settings. This is not just about navigating personal ambitions and interactions; it's about cultivating a culture that fosters collaboration, innovation, and resilience.

At the core, emotional intelligence in the workplace transforms how leaders lead and how teams collaborate. It involves recognizing one's own emotions and those of others, managing these emotions effectively, and using this awareness to guide decision-making and leadership styles. A leader adept in emotional intelligence can inspire and motivate their team, acknowledge and leverage the diverse emotional landscapes of employees, and navigate through times of stress and change with grace and vision.

The application of emotional intelligence at work goes beyond leadership. Team members who understand and manage their emotions contribute to a more positive and productive environment. They can better handle conflicts, provide and receive constructive feedback, and collaborate more effectively. Emotional intelligence fosters an environment where empathy and understanding lead to innovative solutions and where diversity of thought and emotion is celebrated as a strength.

Moreover, emotional intelligence is key in customer and client relations. The ability to empathize with clients, understand their needs, and respond accordingly can set a company apart in today's competitive market. Emotional intelligence empowers employees to deliver exceptional customer service, build strong relationships, and drive customer loyalty, ultimately impacting the bottom line.

In the tapestry of the workplace, the threads of emotional intelligence—self-awareness, self-management, social awareness, and relationship management—interweave to create a stronger, more resilient fabric. This is a workplace where challenges are met with collaborative problem-solving, where the culture thrives on mutual respect and understanding, and where success is measured not just in financial terms but in the growth and well-being of every individual.

Emotional intelligence in the workplace thus extends its benefits far beyond individual success, embodying the essence of holistic prosperity. It is a vital component of thriving professional environments, essential for innovation, productivity, and a positive organizational culture.

## Emotional Intelligence and Mental Health: A Symbiotic Relationship

The intricate dance between emotional intelligence and mental health is one of deep interconnection and mutual enhancement. It's a dynamic interplay where each step of growth in emotional intelligence can lead to strides in mental well-being, and vice versa. This symbiotic relationship underscores not just the importance but the necessity of nurturing our emotional competencies as a pathway to mental resilience and health.

Diving deeper into this relationship, it becomes evident that the components of emotional intelligence—self-awareness, self-management, social awareness, and relationship management —serve as critical tools in managing the complexities of our mental landscapes. For instance, self-awareness offers us a clearer understanding of our emotional triggers and their impact on our thoughts and actions, allowing us to navigate through our mental processes with greater clarity and control. This heightened awareness is a beacon during moments of psychological turmoil, guiding us back to a state of balance and equanimity.

Similarly, the practice of self-management equips us with the strategies to regulate our emotional responses, serving as a buffer against the waves of stress, anxiety, and depression that can often overwhelm us. By mastering our emotional responses, we can maintain a steady course even in the face of life's uncertainties and challenges, reinforcing our mental health and fortitude.

On the social front, empathy and understanding—the hallmarks of social awareness—foster connections that are imbued with mutual support and understanding. These connections are the lifelines that often rescue us from the isolation that mental health struggles can impose, reminding us of our shared humanity and the comfort found in collective resilience.

Lastly, adept relationship management, with its emphasis on communication and conflict resolution, creates an environment where emotional support thrives, further reinforcing our mental well-being. Healthy relationships provide a supportive network that can catch us when we falter, offering both a safe haven and a source of strength as we navigate our mental health journeys.

This symbiotic relationship between emotional intelligence and mental health illuminates the profound impact that cultivating emotional skills can have on our overall psychological well-being. By intentionally developing these competencies, we not only enhance our personal quality of life but also contribute to a broader culture of mental health awareness and support. In this light, emotional intelligence and mental health are not merely interconnected; they are foundational to each other, each fostering growth and healing in a cycle of continuous enrichment.

# Enhancing Emotional Intelligence: Practical Steps and Strategies

To elevate one's emotional intelligence, embarking on a journey of mindful awareness and deliberate practice is essential. Mindfulness, the art of being present and fully engaged with the here and now, offers a powerful tool for tuning into our emotional states and those of others. By adopting mindfulness techniques, such as focused breathing or meditation, individuals can cultivate a heightened sense of awareness that illuminates the intricate dance of thoughts and emotions within.

Self-reflection is another pivotal strategy in the quest to enhance emotional intelligence. This involves setting aside time for introspection to dissect our emotional responses and understand the origins and impacts of these reactions. Such reflective practices can unearth insights into our deepest motivations, fears, and desires, allowing for a richer, more nuanced understanding of ourselves and our interactions with the world.

Active listening, a skill often overlooked, is fundamental in developing empathy and social awareness. It's not merely about hearing the words spoken by others but fully engaging with their message, both verbal and non-verbal. Through active listening, we signal our respect and openness to others' perspectives, fostering deeper connections and mutual understanding.

Embracing a growth mindset, the belief that our abilities and intelligence can be developed over time, encourages resilience in the face of challenges and setbacks. This mindset propels us to view every experience as an opportunity to learn and grow, rather than as a fixed marker of our capabilities.

Seeking and thoughtfully processing feedback from trusted friends, family, or colleagues is invaluable for recognizing blind spots in our emotional awareness and management. Such feedback, when approached with openness and a willingness to grow, can highlight areas for improvement and guide our personal development journey.

Incorporating regular self-care practices, from physical activities like exercise to mental exercises such as journaling, supports emotional wellbeing and resilience. These activities not only improve our physical health but also provide an outlet for processing emotions, reducing stress, and fostering a positive state of mind.

By dedicating oneself to these practical steps and strategies, the path to enhancing emotional intelligence becomes not just a possibility but a rewarding expedition toward greater self-understanding, improved relationships, and a more empathetic engagement with the world.

## The Ripple Effect of Emotional Intelligence: Societal and Global Impact

The transformative power of emotional intelligence extends far beyond the confines of personal growth, casting a wide net of influence that touches every aspect of society. As individuals embark on the journey to enhance their emotional competencies, they inadvertently become catalysts for change, driving forward a culture rooted in empathy, understanding, and mutual respect. This profound shift in interpersonal dynamics has the potential to redefine societal norms, breaking down barriers of miscommunication and conflict that have long hindered collective progress.

In the realm of global impact, the spread of emotional intelligence fosters a new era of international relations and diplomacy. Leaders equipped with the tools of empathy and self-awareness are better positioned to navigate the complexities of cultural differences and global challenges, paving the way for more collaborative and peaceful solutions to the world's most pressing issues. Communities that embrace these principles become beacons of hope, showcasing the tangible benefits of a society built on the foundational pillars of emotional intelligence.

Moreover, the emphasis on relationship management and social awareness nurtures environments where inclusivity and equality flourish. By recognizing and valuing the emotional experiences of every individual, we lay the groundwork for a more equitable world, where every voice is heard, and every person is seen. This collective embrace of emotional intelligence becomes a powerful engine for social change, propelling us towards a future where compassion and understanding are not just ideals, but lived realities.

Thus, the journey towards enhancing emotional intelligence is not a solitary endeavor but a shared voyage that holds the promise of a more harmonious and prosperous global community. It is through this lens that we begin to appreciate the vast potential of emotional intelligence, not only as a tool for personal development but as a key to unlocking a brighter, more connected future for all.

## Strategies for Managing Overwhelming Emotions

Navigating through the stormy seas of overwhelming emotions requires a well-equipped arsenal of strategies, honed for calming the tempest within. It's not merely about weathering the emotional storm, but learning to steer through it with skill and grace. Deep breathing stands as a fundamental technique, serving not just as an anchor but as a means to reset our emotional state. By focusing on the rhythm of our breath, we can induce a state of calmness, signaling to our brain that we are in a safe space, thereby diminishing the intensity of our emotional reactions.

Mindfulness, another vital strategy, invites us to immerse ourselves fully in the present moment, free from the tendrils of past regrets or future anxieties. It teaches us to observe our emotions without judgment, recognizing them as temporary states that ebb and flow. This perspective allows us to detach from the overwhelming intensity of our feelings and approach our emotional landscape with a sense of curiosity and openness.

Cognitive reframing introduces a powerful shift in our approach to challenging emotions. It encourages us to reevaluate our perceptions of stressful situations, transforming them from insurmountable obstacles into opportunities for growth and learning. This technique does not change the external circumstances, but it empowers us to alter our internal dialogue, fostering resilience in the face of adversity.

Together, these strategies offer a multifaceted approach to managing overwhelming emotions. By practicing deep breathing to ground ourselves, adopting mindfulness to stay present, and employing cognitive reframing to shift our perspective, we equip ourselves with the tools necessary for emotional regulation. This suite of techniques not only helps in tempering immediate emotional upheavals but also lays the groundwork for developing long-term emotional resilience, enabling us to face life's challenges with a fortified spirit and a composed heart.

## Cultivating Emotional Resilience

Cultivating emotional resilience is akin to fortifying a castle, preparing it to withstand the inevitable sieges of life. This process involves an intentional effort to strengthen our inner resources, ensuring we can recover from setbacks and adapt to change with agility and grace. The essence of building emotional resilience lies not in avoiding adversity but in engaging with it constructively, allowing ourselves to learn and grow from the challenges we encounter.

At the core of emotional resilience is the development of robust coping mechanisms. These are the strategies we deploy to navigate the emotional turbulence of life's storms. They might include seeking solace in nature, engaging in physical activity to clear the mind, or turning to creative outlets to express what words cannot. Each person's coping mechanisms are as unique as their fingerprints, tailored to their preferences and what brings them peace and perspective.

Another pillar of emotional resilience is the active pursuit of support networks. Humans are inherently social creatures, and our connections with others play a pivotal role in our ability to weather emotional upheavals. Reaching out to friends, family, or support groups provides a safety net of understanding and empathy, reminding us that we are not alone in our struggles.

Practicing self-care is also integral to nurturing emotional resilience. This goes beyond the occasional indulgence to encompass a consistent practice of attending to our physical, emotional, and spiritual needs. It's about recognizing when we need to slow down, recharge, and give ourselves the same compassion and patience we offer to others.

By committing to these practices, we lay the foundations for a resilient spirit. Emotional resilience does not mean being impervious to pain or hardship but possessing the strength and flexibility to rise from the ashes of adversity, armed with newfound wisdom and an unbreakable resolve.

# Enhancing Emotional Intelligence through Empathy

Empathy, an essential facet of emotional intelligence, is the bridge that connects us to the hearts and minds of others. It's the ability to step into someone else's shoes, to view the world through their lens, and to feel what they feel. This profound connection goes beyond mere understanding; it is about sharing in the emotional experiences of others, whether joy, sorrow, or anything in between.

Cultivating empathy is akin to nurturing a garden; it requires patience, care, and a genuine curiosity about the people around us. It begins with active listening, a practice where we give our full attention to the person speaking, absorbing not just their words but the emotions and intentions behind them. This level of attentiveness signals to others that their feelings are valued and understood, laying the groundwork for deeper emotional bonds.

Moreover, empathy extends into the realm of nonverbal communication. It's about being attuned to the subtle cues—facial expressions, body language, and tone of voice—that convey so much more than words alone. By being sensitive to these nonverbal signals, we can respond with greater emotional congruence, fostering an environment of mutual respect and understanding.

To enhance our empathic abilities, we must also engage in self-reflection, recognizing our own biases and preconceptions that may cloud our ability to fully empathize with others. This introspective journey not only broadens our emotional repertoire but also strengthens our capacity for compassion, allowing us to approach each interaction with an open heart and mind.

Empathy, therefore, is not just a tool for improving our relationships; it's a vehicle for transformation, driving us towards a more empathetic, connected, and emotionally intelligent society. By committing to the practice of empathy, we pave the way for a world where understanding reigns, and emotional barriers are dismantled, one heartfelt connection at a time.

# Effective Communication: Expressing Emotions Constructively

Navigating the art of effective communication requires the careful expression of our emotions in a way that is both authentic and mindful of others. It's a dance between transparency and tact, where the objective is not only to convey our feelings but to do so in a manner that fosters understanding and respect. This delicate balance is essential, as it allows us to share our inner world without inadvertently alienating or overwhelming the listener.

Mastering this form of communication demands a certain level of self-awareness. It begins with the recognition and acceptance of our emotions, followed by an evaluation of the most constructive way to express them. This might mean taking a moment to pause and reflect on our feelings before speaking, ensuring that our words are chosen with care and intention. It's about framing our emotions in language that is clear and specific, avoiding vague or charged statements that might lead to confusion or defensiveness.

At the same time, effective communication is a two-way street, requiring an openness to the emotions and perspectives of others. It involves active listening, a willingness to consider feedback, and the flexibility to adapt our approach based on the dynamics of the conversation. This reciprocal engagement enriches the exchange, making it more likely that both parties feel heard, understood, and valued.

Furthermore, the context in which we communicate plays a critical role in how our emotions are received. Being mindful of timing, setting, and the nature of our relationship with the listener can greatly influence the outcome of the conversation. By taking these factors into account, we enhance our ability to express our emotions in a way that is constructive and conducive to positive interactions.

In essence, effective communication about our emotions is an intricate skill that lies at the heart of meaningful connections. It is a testament to the power of emotional intelligence in enriching our interactions and deepening our relationships.

# The Role of Emotional Intelligence in Conflict Resolution

In the arena of conflict resolution, the nuanced application of emotional intelligence becomes a linchpin for navigating through tumultuous interactions with grace and strategic insight. Harnessing emotional intelligence during disagreements empowers us to approach situations from a place of empathy and understanding, elevating our perspective beyond the immediate fray to encompass the broader emotional dynamics at play.

The critical first step in employing emotional intelligence in these scenarios involves recognizing and regulating our own emotions. This self-awareness allows us to maintain composure, ensuring that our responses are measured and thoughtful rather than reactive. By modeling this level of emotional regulation, we set the stage for a more constructive dialogue, inviting all parties to engage in a manner that prioritizes mutual respect over conflict escalation.

A key component of emotional intelligence in this context is the ability to accurately perceive and empathize with the emotions of others. This empathetic attunement enables us to understand the underlying concerns and needs that may be fueling the conflict. With this understanding, we can tailor our communication to address these deeper issues, fostering a sense of validation and understanding that can pave the way for collaborative problem-solving.

Moreover, emotional intelligence equips us with the skills to navigate the delicate balance between standing firm on important issues and demonstrating flexibility where compromise is possible. It involves discerning the right moments to assert our perspective and when to offer concessions, all while keeping the ultimate goal of resolution and relationship preservation in sight.

Engaging emotional intelligence in conflict resolution thus transforms potential adversarial encounters into opportunities for growth and connection. It underscores the power of approaching conflicts not as battles to be won, but as challenges to be understood and resolved through collective empathy and strategic emotional navigation.

## Integrating Emotional Intelligence into Leadership

Incorporating emotional intelligence into the fabric of leadership transforms the very essence of how leaders guide, inspire, and shape their teams. Leaders with a high degree of emotional intelligence possess the unique ability to tune into the emotional undercurrents of their environment, fostering a climate of trust, respect, and open communication. This attunement enables them to address concerns proactively, mediate conflicts with a nuanced understanding of the emotions involved, and inspire collective enthusiasm toward shared goals.

The practice of emotional intelligence in leadership goes beyond mere empathy; it involves a strategic blend of self-awareness, self-regulation, and social skills. Leaders must first navigate their own emotional landscapes with finesse—recognizing their triggers, managing stress effectively, and staying grounded in the face of adversity. This self-mastery not only sets a powerful example for their teams but also equips leaders with the clarity and calm needed to make decisions that are empathetic yet driven by the collective vision.

Socially, emotionally intelligent leaders excel in building and nurturing relationships. They leverage their deep understanding of emotional dynamics to connect with team members on a personal level, recognizing individual strengths and areas for growth. Such leaders adeptly balance giving constructive feedback with championing the successes of their team, cultivating an environment where every member feels valued and understood.

By embedding emotional intelligence into leadership practices, leaders unlock the potential to transform organizational culture. They create spaces where innovation is encouraged, diversity is celebrated, and resilience is built. In doing so, they not only elevate the performance and satisfaction of their teams but also steer their organizations toward sustained success in an ever-evolving world.

## Measuring and Improving Your Emotional Intelligence

Embarking on the journey of enhancing one's emotional intelligence starts with a deliberate and introspective look into our own capabilities and areas ripe for growth. This endeavor requires an honest self-assessment, a willingness to solicit and digest feedback from others, and a commitment to ongoing personal development. Initiating this process involves a careful examination of how we perceive, use, understand, and manage our emotions, as well as how adeptly we navigate the emotional landscapes of those around us.

One effective approach is to engage in structured emotional intelligence training programs or workshops, which can provide valuable insights and practical strategies for improvement. These educational experiences are designed to sharpen our awareness, expand our emotional vocabulary, and enhance our ability to apply emotional knowledge in a variety of situations.

Additionally, seeking out mentorship or coaching from individuals who exemplify high levels of emotional intelligence can offer personalized guidance and support. These relationships serve as a mirror, reflecting our emotional habits and patterns, and providing actionable advice on how to adjust and refine our responses.

Practicing emotional regulation techniques, such as mindfulness meditation, journaling, or cognitive-behavioral strategies, is also vital. These practices help in building a more resilient and responsive emotional framework, enabling us to handle stress and adversity with greater poise and to cultivate a deeper sense of empathy and connection with others.

In essence, improving emotional intelligence is a dynamic and continuous process, one that enriches not only our personal well-being but also enhances our interactions and relationships with others.

# CHAPTER 4: EMPATHY: THE HEART OF EMOTIONAL INTELLIGENCE IN RELATIONSHIPS

In the realm of human relationships, empathy stands as the cornerstone of emotional intelligence. It is the ability to understand and share the feelings of others, fostering deeper connections and more meaningful interactions. In this chapter, we delve into the essence of empathy and its crucial role in cultivating strong, healthy relationships.

## Unveiling the Essence of Empathy in Human Connections

Empathy, often perceived as the heartbeat of our interactions, operates as the pivotal force behind the depth and quality of our human connections. It transcends mere understanding, venturing into the realm of deeply sharing and experiencing the emotional states of others. This profound connection fosters a unique bond, a silent acknowledgment that we are not alone in our experiences, enhancing our sense of belonging and shared human condition.

At its core, empathy is about vulnerability and courage—the willingness to open ourselves up to not only recognize but also feel the emotions of another person. This act of emotional bravery does more than just bridge the gap between individuals; it serves as a testament to our inherent interconnectedness. Through empathy, we not only offer comfort but also receive insights and understanding, enriching our own emotional landscapes.

Empathy does not demand that we have lived the exact experiences of others but requires the openness to inhabit their emotional world, viewing their circumstances through a lens of compassion and understanding. This journey into another's emotional experience is guided by our innate capacity for emotional resonance, allowing us to connect on a level that words often cannot reach.

By nurturing our empathetic abilities, we unlock the potential for more genuine and profound connections. It is through empathy that we can truly appreciate the complexities of human emotion, celebrating our differences and finding common ground in our shared humanity. In doing so, empathy lays the groundwork for relationships that are not only more compassionate but also more resilient in the face of adversity.

As we venture further into exploring empathy's role in our lives, it becomes clear that it is not just a skill to be developed but a gift to be cherished. Empathy, in its purest form, has the power to transform our interactions, turning fleeting encounters into lasting bonds and creating a world where emotional understanding and compassion are the norm.

## The Science Behind Empathy: Understanding Its Roots

Neuroscience provides us with a fascinating window into how empathy works within the brain, illuminating the complex networks and processes that enable us to feel and understand the emotions of others. At the heart of this scientific exploration is the discovery of mirror neurons, a type of brain cell that reacts both when we perform an action and when we observe the same action performed by someone else. This mirroring mechanism is crucial for empathy, as it allows us to literally feel a reflection of others' emotions within ourselves, providing a biological basis for our capacity to empathize.

Further research into the neural underpinnings of empathy has identified specific regions of the brain, such as the insula and the anterior cingulate cortex, that are activated when we engage in empathetic processing. These areas are involved in the emotional aspects of empathy, helping us to not only recognize but also vicariously experience the feelings of others. Such findings underscore empathy's role as an integral part of our social cognition, facilitating not just personal relationships but also our survival as a social species.

The interplay between these neural networks and our own emotional experiences highlights the deeply ingrained nature of empathy in the human psyche. It is not merely a learned behavior but a fundamental part of our neurological makeup. However, the extent and manner in which we express empathy can be influenced by our life experiences, culture, and individual differences, suggesting that while the capacity for empathy is universal, its expression is uniquely personal.

Understanding the science behind empathy not only deepens our appreciation for this critical aspect of human interaction but also opens the door to enhancing our empathetic abilities. By recognizing that empathy has roots in the very structure of our brains, we can begin to see it as a natural, essential part of what it means to be human, further motivating us to cultivate this trait within ourselves and our communities.

## Emotional Intelligence: The Framework for Empathetic Engagement

Emotional intelligence (EI) serves as the scaffolding upon which our capacity for empathy is built and nurtured. It involves a nuanced mastery of recognizing, understanding, and managing our own emotions, while simultaneously being attuned to the emotions of those around us. At the heart of emotional intelligence lies the ability to perceive emotions accurately, both in ourselves and in others. This perception acts as the first step toward empathetic engagement, enabling us to navigate the intricate dance of human interaction with grace and awareness.

The journey of emotional intelligence unfolds through self-awareness, inviting us into a deeper understanding of our emotional responses and how they influence our thoughts and actions. This internal compass is invaluable, as it guides our steps toward self-regulation, the ability to manage and adjust our emotions in a way that aligns with our highest intentions. As we cultivate these internal skills, our focus shifts outward to social awareness— the skill of recognizing and understanding the emotions of others. This outward focus is where empathy takes root, allowing us to resonate with others on an emotional level.

Engaging empathetically with others also demands the practice of relationship management, a cornerstone of emotional intelligence. It encompasses our ability to inspire, influence, and develop others while managing conflict and fostering strong, healthy relationships. Herein lies the power of emotional intelligence as a framework for empathetic engagement; it equips us with the tools to not only understand and share the feelings of others but also to navigate the complexities of human relationships with a kind and compassionate hand.

As we refine these emotional intelligence skills, our interactions become more meaningful and enriched, marked by a genuine connection that transcends the superficial. Through emotional intelligence, we unlock a more authentic, empathetic way of relating to the world and the people within it, paving the way for deeper, more rewarding connections.

## Listening with Intent: The Gateway to Empathy

Active listening stands as a vital skill in the realm of empathy, serving as a bridge to truly grasp the perspectives and feelings of those we interact with. When we listen with intent, we're not merely waiting for our turn to speak, but deeply engaging with the words and emotions being shared with us. This form of listening goes beyond the auditory experience to involve a full, undivided presence, signaling to the speaker that they are valued and their experiences genuinely matter to us.

Engaging in active listening requires a conscious effort to set aside our own thoughts, judgments, and the impulse to provide immediate solutions. Instead, it demands that we immerse ourselves in the narrative of the other, accompanying them in their emotional journey. Such attentive listening fosters a profound sense of understanding and validation, building the foundation for a trust-filled relationship. It's about acknowledging the silent messages between words, the pauses, and the unspoken emotions conveyed through tone and expression.

This process of tuning in with empathy allows us to perceive the world from another's vantage point, enriching our emotional intelligence by broadening our understanding of the diverse tapestry of human experience. By focusing on the person in front of us, we open ourselves to a deeper level of emotional connection, one that transcends mere conversation and touches the essence of human connection.

Moreover, active listening embodies the respect and care we have for others. It communicates that we are willing to be moved by their experiences, to be influenced by their emotions, and to engage in a shared emotional space. This level of engagement is transformative, not just for the individual being heard but for the listener as well, as it deepens our capacity for empathy and fosters a sense of communal understanding and support.

In cultivating our ability to listen with intent, we unlock the gateway to empathy, ushering in more authentic and compassionate interactions. Through this practice, we learn not just to hear, but to truly understand and connect with the hearts and minds of those around us, strengthening the bonds that bind us as human beings.

The nuanced dance of non-verbal communication plays an indispensable role in the art of empathy. Beyond the words we speak, it is through facial expressions, body language, and the subtleties of tone that the true depth of our feelings often emerges. These silent signals serve as a powerful conduit for emotional understanding, offering a window into the unspoken truths of the human experience.

In the realm of empathetic interactions, the ability to interpret and respond to non-verbal cues is paramount. A furrowed brow, a hesitant pause, or a softening of the eyes can communicate volumes, revealing layers of emotion that words alone may fail to capture. By attuning ourselves to these subtle expressions, we bridge the gap between mere conversation and true connection, enabling a richer, more nuanced exchange of empathy.

Engaging with non-verbal communication demands a presence of mind and an openness of heart. It requires us to be fully immersed in the moment, to listen not just with our ears but with our whole being. This level of engagement allows us to resonate with others on a visceral level, facilitating a form of emotional communion that transcends language.

As we navigate our interactions, paying mindful attention to the non-verbal cues of those around us enriches our understanding and enhances our empathetic capacity. It empowers us to respond with sensitivity and compassion, fostering an environment where genuine emotional exchange can flourish. In doing so, we affirm the value of every gesture, glance, and sigh, honoring the complexity of human emotion and the profound connections that arise when we communicate from the heart.

# Empathy in Action: Practical Steps to Improve Your Empathetic Abilities

Developing a keen sense of empathy involves more than just understanding its importance; it requires deliberate practice and intentionality in our daily interactions. One foundational step is to cultivate a mindset of curiosity about the people around us. This means asking open-ended questions that encourage others to express their thoughts and feelings, and genuinely being interested in their responses. By doing so, we not only learn about their experiences but also demonstrate our willingness to understand their perspective.

Another practical approach is to actively engage in perspective-taking. Try to put yourself in someone else's shoes, imagining their emotional experience as if it were your own. This can be facilitated through reading diverse narratives or engaging in role-play exercises that challenge you to adopt viewpoints different from your own. Such exercises not only enhance your ability to empathize but also expand your emotional vocabulary, enabling you to articulate feelings more accurately.

Mindful listening is also crucial. This involves giving your full attention to the speaker, without formulating your response while they are talking. Notice not only what is being said but how it is being expressed. Pay attention to non-verbal cues such as body language and tone of voice, which can provide deeper insights into the speaker's emotional state.

Additionally, reflecting on your own emotional experiences and how they influence your reactions to others can greatly enhance your empathetic abilities. Engaging in regular self-reflection helps you to recognize your emotional triggers and biases, making it easier to separate your feelings from those of others when practicing empathy.

Lastly, seek feedback on your interactions. Inviting others to share how they felt during your conversations can offer valuable insights into your empathetic strengths and areas for improvement. Through consistent practice, these steps can significantly bolster your ability to connect with others on a deeper, more empathetic level.

## The Impact of Empathy on Relationships: Personal and Professional

Empathy weaves itself into the fabric of our relationships, acting as a linchpin for building connections that are not just enduring but also enriching. In personal relationships, empathy serves as a bridge to understanding, allowing us to navigate the complexities of human emotions with grace and compassion. It's through this profound understanding that we cultivate deeper connections with our loved ones, transforming everyday interactions into opportunities for genuine connection and growth.

In the professional realm, empathy is equally transformative. It underpins effective leadership and teamwork, fostering an environment where communication thrives and diverse perspectives are valued. Empathy in the workplace leads to a culture of trust and respect, where conflicts become constructive and collaboration is the norm. It's not just about achieving organizational goals but about creating a workspace where individuals feel understood and valued, enhancing job satisfaction and productivity.

Integrating empathy into our personal and professional lives demands intentional practice. It involves actively listening, being present, and consistently seeking to understand the perspectives and feelings of others. This practice not only enriches our interactions but also strengthens our emotional intelligence, allowing us to navigate relationships with a nuanced understanding of the emotional landscapes we encounter.

Empathy's impact is far-reaching, touching every aspect of our relationships. It encourages openness, facilitates healing, and promotes a shared sense of humanity. Whether in intimate personal connections or in the broader context of our professional lives, empathy stands as a testament to our capacity for kindness, understanding, and profound connection. By valuing and practicing empathy, we not only enrich our own lives but also contribute to a more compassionate and connected world.

## Navigating Emotional Boundaries While Practicing Empathy

In the journey of deepening our empathetic connections, it's imperative to recognize the importance of establishing emotional boundaries. This nuanced balancing act ensures that while we open our hearts to the emotions of others, we don't lose sight of our own well-being. Emotional boundaries allow us to empathize without adopting the weight of others' emotions as our own burden. This delineation is critical, for it enables us to offer support and understanding without compromising our emotional health.

Creating and maintaining these boundaries begins with self-awareness. By understanding our emotional triggers and limits, we can better identify when we are at risk of overextending ourselves. It's about acknowledging that empathy does not require us to dissolve into the emotional experiences of others but to stand beside them, offering support while remaining anchored in our own emotional reality.

This practice also involves clear communication, articulating our needs and limitations to others. It's a declaration of our commitment to empathy, paired with an understanding of our capacity. This transparency fosters a mutual respect for emotional boundaries, paving the way for healthier, more sustainable interactions.

Engaging in regular self-reflection is another vital component. It encourages us to examine how our empathetic engagements affect us emotionally and to adjust our boundaries as needed. This ongoing process ensures that our empathetic endeavors remain nourishing rather than depleting.

Ultimately, the art of navigating emotional boundaries while practicing empathy is a testament to our commitment to both our own well-being and that of those around us. It underscores the belief that true empathy is not about losing ourselves in the emotions of others but about connecting with them in a way that is respectful and mindful of the emotional landscapes of all involved.

## Empathy Burnout: Recognizing and Managing the Risks

While empathy is a vital component of deep, meaningful relationships, it is crucial to recognize the potential for empathy burnout. This form of exhaustion occurs when continuous emotional engagement with others' pain and distress surpasses our capacity to recharge, leading to a state where one's empathy well runs dry. Characterized by feelings of numbness, irritability, and a diminished capacity to empathize, burnout not only affects our ability to connect with others but also our overall well-being.

To navigate these waters safely, it's imperative to cultivate strategies for self-preservation alongside our empathetic practices. One effective approach is setting firm emotional boundaries, an act that allows us to remain compassionate without absorbing the emotional turmoil of others. It's about learning to say "no" or "not now" when we find ourselves nearing our limits, ensuring that we do not compromise our mental health for the sake of being perpetually available.

Moreover, incorporating regular self-care routines acts as a counterbalance to the heavy lifting involved in empathetic interactions. Whether it's engaging in physical activity, pursuing hobbies, or practicing mindfulness, these activities can replenish our emotional reserves, making us more resilient and less susceptible to burnout.

Additionally, seeking support through dialogue with trusted friends or professionals can offer fresh perspectives and coping strategies. Sharing our experiences can lighten the load, reminding us that we are not alone in our efforts to navigate the complexities of empathy.

Embracing these practices enables us to sustain our empathetic engagement over the long term, ensuring that we can continue to offer support to others while maintaining our emotional health. This balanced approach is key to preventing empathy burnout, allowing us to thrive in both our personal and professional lives.

## The Future of Empathy: Cultivating Compassionate Societies

In envisioning a future where empathy shapes our societies, we're drawn to the transformative potential of collective compassion. This vision hinges on integrating empathetic understanding into the fabric of our communities, encouraging a shift towards more considerate interactions and decision-making processes. Elevating empathy in this way promises not only to enhance the quality of our personal relationships but also to influence broader societal structures, from education systems to workplaces, fostering environments that prioritize emotional intelligence alongside traditional metrics of success.

The key to achieving this lies in nurturing empathy from a young age, instilling values of kindness and understanding in the next generation. Educational initiatives that incorporate emotional intelligence training can play a pivotal role, equipping young minds with the tools necessary for empathetic engagement. Similarly, workplaces that champion empathy as a core value contribute to a culture of mutual respect, where employees feel seen and valued, promoting not just productivity but also a sense of communal well-being.

By collectively committing to these principles, we pave the way for a future where empathy is not an afterthought but a foundational pillar of society. This commitment promises to bridge divides, heal wounds, and usher in an era of heightened communal harmony, illustrating the profound impact empathy can have when embraced on a global scale.

# CHAPTER 5: EMPATHY: THE HEART OF EMOTIONAL INTELLIGENCE IN RELATIONSHIPS

In the realm of human relationships, empathy stands as the cornerstone of emotional intelligence. It is the ability to understand and share the feelings of others, fostering deeper connections and more meaningful interactions. In this chapter, we delve into the essence of empathy and its crucial role in cultivating strong, healthy relationships.

## Unveiling the Essence of Empathy in Human Connections

Empathy, often perceived as the heartbeat of our interactions, operates as the pivotal force behind the depth and quality of our human connections. It transcends mere understanding, venturing into the realm of deeply sharing and experiencing the emotional states of others. This profound connection fosters a unique bond, a silent acknowledgment that we are not alone in our experiences, enhancing our sense of belonging and shared human condition.

At its core, empathy is about vulnerability and courage—the willingness to open ourselves up to not only recognize but also feel the emotions of another person. This act of emotional bravery does more than just bridge the gap between individuals; it serves as a testament to our inherent interconnectedness. Through empathy, we not only offer comfort but also receive insights and understanding, enriching our own emotional landscapes.

Empathy does not demand that we have lived the exact experiences of others but requires the openness to inhabit their emotional world, viewing their circumstances through a lens of compassion and understanding. This journey into another's emotional experience is guided by our innate capacity for emotional resonance, allowing us to connect on a level that words often cannot reach.

By nurturing our empathetic abilities, we unlock the potential for more genuine and profound connections. It is through empathy that we can truly appreciate the complexities of human emotion, celebrating our differences and finding common ground in our shared humanity. In doing so, empathy lays the groundwork for relationships that are not only more compassionate but also more resilient in the face of adversity.

As we venture further into exploring empathy's role in our lives, it becomes clear that it is not just a skill to be developed but a gift to be cherished. Empathy, in its purest form, has the power to transform our interactions, turning fleeting encounters into lasting bonds and creating a world where emotional understanding and compassion are the norm.

# The Science Behind Empathy: Understanding Its Roots

Neuroscience provides us with a fascinating window into how empathy works within the brain, illuminating the complex networks and processes that enable us to feel and understand the emotions of others. At the heart of this scientific exploration is the discovery of mirror neurons, a type of brain cell that reacts both when we perform an action and when we observe the same action performed by someone else. This mirroring mechanism is crucial for empathy, as it allows us to literally feel a reflection of others' emotions within ourselves, providing a biological basis for our capacity to empathize.

Further research into the neural underpinnings of empathy has identified specific regions of the brain, such as the insula and the anterior cingulate cortex, that are activated when we engage in empathetic processing. These areas are involved in the emotional aspects of empathy, helping us to not only recognize but also vicariously experience the feelings of others. Such findings underscore empathy's role as an integral part of our social cognition, facilitating not just personal relationships but also our survival as a social species.

The interplay between these neural networks and our own emotional experiences highlights the deeply ingrained nature of empathy in the human psyche. It is not merely a learned behavior but a fundamental part of our neurological makeup. However, the extent and manner in which we express empathy can be influenced by our life experiences, culture, and individual differences, suggesting that while the capacity for empathy is universal, its expression is uniquely personal.

Understanding the science behind empathy not only deepens our appreciation for this critical aspect of human interaction but also opens the door to enhancing our empathetic abilities. By recognizing that empathy has roots in the very structure of our brains, we can begin to see it as a natural, essential part of what it means to be human, further motivating us to cultivate this trait within ourselves and our communities.

# Emotional Intelligence: The Framework for Empathetic Engagement

Emotional intelligence (EI) serves as the scaffolding upon which our capacity for empathy is built and nurtured. It involves a nuanced mastery of recognizing, understanding, and managing our own emotions, while simultaneously being attuned to the emotions of those around us. At the heart of emotional intelligence lies the ability to perceive emotions accurately, both in ourselves and in others. This perception acts as the first step toward empathetic engagement, enabling us to navigate the intricate dance of human interaction with grace and awareness.

The journey of emotional intelligence unfolds through self-awareness, inviting us into a deeper understanding of our emotional responses and how they influence our thoughts and actions. This internal compass is invaluable, as it guides our steps toward self-regulation, the ability to manage and adjust our emotions in a way that aligns with our highest intentions. As we cultivate these internal skills, our focus shifts outward to social awareness— the skill of recognizing and understanding the emotions of others. This outward focus is where empathy takes root, allowing us to resonate with others on an emotional level.

Engaging empathetically with others also demands the practice of relationship management, a cornerstone of emotional intelligence. It encompasses our ability to inspire, influence, and develop others while managing conflict and fostering strong, healthy relationships. Herein lies the power of emotional intelligence as a framework for empathetic engagement; it equips us with the tools to not only understand and share the feelings of others but also to navigate the complexities of human relationships with a kind and compassionate hand.

As we refine these emotional intelligence skills, our interactions become more meaningful and enriched, marked by a genuine connection that transcends the superficial. Through emotional intelligence, we unlock a more authentic, empathetic way of relating to the world and the people within it, paving the way for deeper, more rewarding connections.

## Listening with Intent: The Gateway to Empathy

Active listening stands as a vital skill in the realm of empathy, serving as a bridge to truly grasp the perspectives and feelings of those we interact with. When we listen with intent, we're not merely waiting for our turn to speak, but deeply engaging with the words and emotions being shared with us. This form of listening goes beyond the auditory experience to involve a full, undivided presence, signaling to the speaker that they are valued and their experiences genuinely matter to us.

Engaging in active listening requires a conscious effort to set aside our own thoughts, judgments, and the impulse to provide immediate solutions. Instead, it demands that we immerse ourselves in the narrative of the other, accompanying them in their emotional journey. Such attentive listening fosters a profound sense of understanding and validation, building the foundation for a trust-filled relationship. It's about acknowledging the silent messages between words, the pauses, and the unspoken emotions conveyed through tone and expression.

This process of tuning in with empathy allows us to perceive the world from another's vantage point, enriching our emotional intelligence by broadening our understanding of the diverse tapestry of human experience. By focusing on the person in front of us, we open ourselves to a deeper level of emotional connection, one that transcends mere conversation and touches the essence of human connection.

Moreover, active listening embodies the respect and care we have for others. It communicates that we are willing to be moved by their experiences, to be influenced by their emotions, and to engage in a shared emotional space. This level of engagement is transformative, not just for the individual being heard but for the listener as well, as it deepens our capacity for empathy and fosters a sense of communal understanding and support.

In cultivating our ability to listen with intent, we unlock the gateway to empathy, ushering in more authentic and compassionate interactions. Through this practice, we learn not just to hear, but to truly understand and connect with the hearts and minds of those around us, strengthening the bonds that bind us as human beings.

## The Role of Non-Verbal Communication in Empathy

The nuanced dance of non-verbal communication plays an indispensable role in the art of empathy. Beyond the words we speak, it is through facial expressions, body language, and the subtleties of tone that the true depth of our feelings often emerges. These silent signals serve as a powerful conduit for emotional understanding, offering a window into the unspoken truths of the human experience.

In the realm of empathetic interactions, the ability to interpret and respond to non-verbal cues is paramount. A furrowed brow, a hesitant pause, or a softening of the eyes can communicate volumes, revealing layers of emotion that words alone may fail to capture. By attuning ourselves to these subtle expressions, we bridge the gap between mere conversation and true connection, enabling a richer, more nuanced exchange of empathy.

Engaging with non-verbal communication demands a presence of mind and an openness of heart. It requires us to be fully immersed in the moment, to listen not just with our ears but with our whole being. This level of engagement allows us to resonate with others on a visceral level, facilitating a form of emotional communion that transcends language.

As we navigate our interactions, paying mindful attention to the non-verbal cues of those around us enriches our understanding and enhances our empathetic capacity. It empowers us to respond with sensitivity and compassion, fostering an environment where genuine emotional exchange can flourish. In doing so, we affirm the value of every gesture, glance, and sigh, honoring the complexity of human emotion and the profound connections that arise when we communicate from the heart.

## Empathy in Action: Practical Steps to Improve Your Empathetic Abilities

Developing a keen sense of empathy involves more than just understanding its importance; it requires deliberate practice and intentionality in our daily interactions. One foundational step is to cultivate a mindset of curiosity about the people around us. This means asking open-ended questions that encourage others to express their thoughts and feelings, and genuinely being interested in their responses. By doing so, we not only learn about their experiences but also demonstrate our willingness to understand their perspective.

Another practical approach is to actively engage in perspective-taking. Try to put yourself in someone else's shoes, imagining their emotional experience as if it were your own. This can be facilitated through reading diverse narratives or engaging in role-play exercises that challenge you to adopt viewpoints different from your own. Such exercises not only enhance your ability to empathize but also expand your emotional vocabulary, enabling you to articulate feelings more accurately.

Mindful listening is also crucial. This involves giving your full attention to the speaker, without formulating your response while they are talking. Notice not only what is being said but how it is being expressed. Pay attention to non-verbal cues such as body language and tone of voice, which can provide deeper insights into the speaker's emotional state.

Additionally, reflecting on your own emotional experiences and how they influence your reactions to others can greatly enhance your empathetic abilities. Engaging in regular self-reflection helps you to recognize your emotional triggers and biases, making it easier to separate your feelings from those of others when practicing empathy.

Lastly, seek feedback on your interactions. Inviting others to share how they felt during your conversations can offer valuable insights into your empathetic strengths and areas for improvement. Through consistent practice, these steps can significantly bolster your ability to connect with others on a deeper, more empathetic level.

# The Impact of Empathy on Relationships: Personal and Professional

Empathy weaves itself into the fabric of our relationships, acting as a linchpin for building connections that are not just enduring but also enriching. In personal relationships, empathy serves as a bridge to understanding, allowing us to navigate the complexities of human emotions with grace and compassion. It's through this profound understanding that we cultivate deeper connections with our loved ones, transforming everyday interactions into opportunities for genuine connection and growth.

In the professional realm, empathy is equally transformative. It underpins effective leadership and teamwork, fostering an environment where communication thrives and diverse perspectives are valued. Empathy in the workplace leads to a culture of trust and respect, where conflicts become constructive and collaboration is the norm. It's not just about achieving organizational goals but about creating a workspace where individuals feel understood and valued, enhancing job satisfaction and productivity.

Integrating empathy into our personal and professional lives demands intentional practice. It involves actively listening, being present, and consistently seeking to understand the perspectives and feelings of others. This practice not only enriches our interactions but also strengthens our emotional intelligence, allowing us to navigate relationships with a nuanced understanding of the emotional landscapes we encounter.

Empathy's impact is far-reaching, touching every aspect of our relationships. It encourages openness, facilitates healing, and promotes a shared sense of humanity. Whether in intimate personal connections or in the broader context of our professional lives, empathy stands as a testament to our capacity for kindness, understanding, and profound connection. By valuing and practicing empathy, we not only enrich our own lives but also contribute to a more compassionate and connected world.

# Navigating Emotional Boundaries While Practicing Empathy

In the journey of deepening our empathetic connections, it's imperative to recognize the importance of establishing emotional boundaries. This nuanced balancing act ensures that while we open our hearts to the emotions of others, we don't lose sight of our own well-being. Emotional boundaries allow us to empathize without adopting the weight of others' emotions as our own burden. This delineation is critical, for it enables us to offer support and understanding without compromising our emotional health.

Creating and maintaining these boundaries begins with self-awareness. By understanding our emotional triggers and limits, we can better identify when we are at risk of overextending ourselves. It's about acknowledging that empathy does not require us to dissolve into the emotional experiences of others but to stand beside them, offering support while remaining anchored in our own emotional reality.

This practice also involves clear communication, articulating our needs and limitations to others. It's a declaration of our commitment to empathy, paired with an understanding of our capacity. This transparency fosters a mutual respect for emotional boundaries, paving the way for healthier, more sustainable interactions.

Engaging in regular self-reflection is another vital component. It encourages us to examine how our empathetic engagements affect us emotionally and to adjust our boundaries as needed. This ongoing process ensures that our empathetic endeavors remain nourishing rather than depleting.

Ultimately, the art of navigating emotional boundaries while practicing empathy is a testament to our commitment to both our own well-being and that of those around us. It underscores the belief that true empathy is not about losing ourselves in the emotions of others but about connecting with them in a way that is respectful and mindful of the emotional landscapes of all involved.

## Empathy Burnout: Recognizing and Managing the Risks

While empathy is a vital component of deep, meaningful relationships, it is crucial to recognize the potential for empathy burnout. This form of exhaustion occurs when continuous emotional engagement with others' pain and distress surpasses our capacity to recharge, leading to a state where one's empathy well runs dry. Characterized by feelings of numbness, irritability, and a diminished capacity to empathize, burnout not only affects our ability to connect with others but also our overall well-being.

To navigate these waters safely, it's imperative to cultivate strategies for self-preservation alongside our empathetic practices. One effective approach is setting firm emotional boundaries, an act that allows us to remain compassionate without absorbing the emotional turmoil of others. It's about learning to say "no" or "not now" when we find ourselves nearing our limits, ensuring that we do not compromise our mental health for the sake of being perpetually available.

Moreover, incorporating regular self-care routines acts as a counterbalance to the heavy lifting involved in empathetic interactions. Whether it's engaging in physical activity, pursuing hobbies, or practicing mindfulness, these activities can replenish our emotional reserves, making us more resilient and less susceptible to burnout.

Additionally, seeking support through dialogue with trusted friends or professionals can offer fresh perspectives and coping strategies. Sharing our experiences can lighten the load, reminding us that we are not alone in our efforts to navigate the complexities of empathy.

Embracing these practices enables us to sustain our empathetic engagement over the long term, ensuring that we can continue to offer support to others while maintaining our emotional health. This balanced approach is key to preventing empathy burnout, allowing us to thrive in both our personal and professional lives.

## The Future of Empathy: Cultivating Compassionate Societies

In envisioning a future where empathy shapes our societies, we're drawn to the transformative potential of collective compassion. This vision hinges on integrating empathetic understanding into the fabric of our communities, encouraging a shift towards more considerate interactions and decision-making processes. Elevating empathy in this way promises not only to enhance the quality of our personal relationships but also to influence broader societal structures, from education systems to workplaces, fostering environments that prioritize emotional intelligence alongside traditional metrics of success.

The key to achieving this lies in nurturing empathy from a young age, instilling values of kindness and understanding in the next generation. Educational initiatives that incorporate emotional intelligence training can play a pivotal role, equipping young minds with the tools necessary for empathetic engagement. Similarly, workplaces that champion empathy as a core value contribute to a culture of mutual respect, where employees feel seen and valued, promoting not just productivity but also a sense of communal well-being.

By collectively committing to these principles, we pave the way for a future where empathy is not an afterthought but a foundational pillar of society. This commitment promises to bridge divides, heal wounds, and usher in an era of heightened communal harmony, illustrating the profound impact empathy can have when embraced on a global scale.

# CHAPTER 6: BOOSTING EMOTIONAL INTELLIGENCE FOR FULFILLING RELATIONSHIPS

Emotional intelligence plays a crucial role in fostering meaningful and fulfilling relationships. Understanding and developing emotional intelligence can significantly enhance our ability to connect with others on a deeper level, leading to stronger bonds and healthier interactions. In this chapter, we will explore the importance of emotional intelligence in relationships and provide practical tips on how to boost it for more fulfilling connections.

## The Role of Active Listening in Enhancing Emotional Connections

Active listening stands as a cornerstone of emotional intelligence, particularly when it comes to strengthening the ties that bind us in our personal relationships. It's not merely about hearing the words that are spoken but engaging fully with the speaker—understanding their message, feeling their emotions, and acknowledging their perspective. This form of listening transcends the conventional; it requires a full immersion into the conversation without the distractions of formulating responses or passing judgment.

When we actively listen, we are committing ourselves to genuinely understand what is being communicated. This involves paying close attention not only to the spoken words but also to the tone of voice, facial expressions, and body language—all of which convey nuanced layers of meaning. It's about creating a supportive environment where the speaker feels valued and understood, a fundamental aspect of fostering emotional connections.

By reflecting on what has been said and asking open-ended questions, we encourage a deeper exploration of thoughts and feelings. This approach not only clarifies our understanding but also validates the speaker's emotions and experiences, making them feel seen and heard. Active listening bridges gaps and heals misunderstandings, serving as a vital tool in nurturing closer, more empathetic relationships.

Implementing active listening in our daily interactions requires patience, practice, and a genuine intention to connect with others on a meaningful level. It's about silencing our inner voice and distractions, focusing entirely on the person in front of us. Such dedication to understanding and empathizing with others paves the way for more profound emotional bonds and a greater sense of closeness and trust. In the realm of emotional intelligence, active listening is not just a skill but a gift we offer to those we care about, enabling us to cultivate relationships that are deeply connected and richly rewarding.

## Empathy: The Heart of Emotional Intelligence

Empathy, a central component of emotional intelligence, goes beyond mere sympathy to involve a profound understanding and sharing of the feelings of another. This capability is essential for nurturing relationships that are not only fulfilling but also resilient and empathetic. To empathize is to dive into the emotional world of another person, to view the situation through their eyes, and to feel what they are feeling as if those emotions were your own. It's a skill that, when effectively utilized, has the power to dissolve barriers and foster a profound connection between individuals.

In practice, empathy involves active engagement and a willingness to be present with another's emotional experience without judgment. It requires a delicate balance of listening, understanding, and responding in a way that conveys solidarity and compassion. When we empathize, we acknowledge the other person's feelings as valid and significant, thereby validating their experience and perspective. This validation is a powerful act of kindness and respect, which strengthens the bonds of trust and mutual respect that are so essential to healthy, lasting relationships.

Moreover, empathy extends its benefits beyond the immediate emotional comfort it provides. It lays the groundwork for deeper, more meaningful interactions and a mutual understanding that can weather the challenges and conflicts inevitable in any relationship. By fostering an environment where individuals feel understood and supported in their emotional experiences, empathy cultivates a fertile ground for growth, healing, and the flourishing of relationships.

Empathy, therefore, is not just about emotional resonance; it's about building a bridge of understanding and compassion that connects us to the people in our lives in a meaningful way. It is through this deep, empathetic connection that we can truly appreciate the richness of human relationships and the transformative impact of emotional intelligence in our lives.

## The Strength in Vulnerability: Opening Up to Deepen Bonds

Opening ourselves up to reveal our true feelings, insecurities, and fears is a powerful act of courage that can dramatically transform our relationships. Vulnerability, far from being a sign of weakness, is a testament to our strength and a gateway to genuine human connection. When we allow ourselves to be vulnerable, we invite others into our inner world, fostering a climate of mutual trust and authenticity. This openness is crucial for developing deeper, more meaningful connections, as it signals to others that they are in a safe space to share their own vulnerabilities.

Vulnerability acts as a catalyst for intimacy, breaking down barriers and dissolving the masks we often wear to protect ourselves. It challenges the notion that we must always appear strong or perfect to be loved, encouraging a more authentic interaction between individuals. By sharing our true selves, we give permission for others to do the same, leading to a richer, more connected experience. This level of emotional exposure can be daunting, yet it is precisely what draws us closer, allowing for a level of understanding and empathy that superficial interactions lack.

In practicing vulnerability, it's vital to choose the right moment and the right person, ensuring a supportive environment that nurtures openness and acceptance. It involves risk, but it is within this risk that we find the opportunity for growth and stronger bonds. By navigating our fears and choosing to be open, we not only enhance our capacity for emotional intelligence but also empower others to embrace their vulnerability. This mutual exchange of authenticity strengthens the fabric of our relationships, making them more resilient and enriched by deep, unwavering trust. Through vulnerability, we discover the true essence of connection and the boundless strength it brings to our relationships.

## Self-Regulation Strategies to Manage Your Emotions

Self-regulation is pivotal in our emotional toolkit, offering a way to navigate the tumultuous seas of our feelings with grace and tact. Mastering self-regulation enables us to pause before responding, providing space to choose actions that align with our best selves and the health of our relationships. Here, we delve into effective strategies to foster this crucial skill.

One foundational approach is mindfulness, which teaches us to observe our emotions without judgment. Through mindfulness practices, such as meditation or focused breathing exercises, we can develop the ability to witness our emotional responses without immediately acting on them. This heightened awareness creates a buffer against impulsive reactions, allowing for more considered and compassionate responses.

Another powerful tool in the self-regulation arsenal is reframing. This involves intentionally shifting our perspective on challenging situations or emotions. By adopting a more positive or neutral viewpoint, we can reduce the intensity of negative emotions and open up pathways to constructive outcomes. For instance, viewing a disagreement as an opportunity for growth rather than a threat can transform the emotional landscape of the interaction.

Setting clear boundaries is also essential for effective self-regulation. Knowing our limits and communicating them respectfully helps prevent emotional overload and maintains our well-being. Boundaries empower us to say no when necessary and choose engagements that support our emotional health.

Engaging in regular physical activity is yet another strategy that can significantly impact our emotional regulation. Exercise not only improves our physical health but also acts as a natural stress reliever. Physical activities, from yoga to running, can help dissipate tension, clear the mind, and elevate our mood, equipping us better to handle emotional challenges.

Incorporating these strategies into our daily lives requires intention and practice. However, the rewards—improved emotional balance, enhanced relationships, and increased personal well-being—are profound. As we refine our self-regulation skills, we become more adept at navigating life's emotional complexities with resilience and empathy.

## Recognizing and Responding to the Emotional Needs of Others

Attuning to the emotional needs of our partners, friends, and family members is a cornerstone of emotional intelligence that enriches relationships. This sensitivity allows us to act with kindness and support, precisely when it's needed most. By observing and understanding the cues that signal someone's emotional state—be it a subtle change in expression, a shift in tone of voice, or certain behavioral patterns—we can respond in ways that are both meaningful and affirming.

To effectively meet the emotional needs of others, we must first cultivate a deep level of empathy, as discussed in previous sections. This involves putting ourselves in their shoes, imagining their feelings, and understanding their perspective without judgment. Armed with this insight, we're better equipped to offer the right kind of support—whether it's words of affirmation, acts of service, or simply being present and listening.

Responding appropriately to the emotional needs of others also means recognizing when to offer advice and when to provide silent support. Sometimes, what's needed most is not a solution but the comfort of knowing they're not alone. It's about striking the right balance between intervening and allowing space for others to express themselves freely.

In practice, this may involve checking in with loved ones regularly, asking open-ended questions that encourage them to share their feelings, or acknowledging their emotions through validation. Phrases like "It sounds like you're really going through a tough time" or "I'm here for you, no matter what" can be incredibly powerful in conveying empathy and understanding.

Engaging with the emotional needs of others in these thoughtful ways not only strengthens the bonds of relationships but also promotes a mutual sense of security and trust. It highlights our commitment to the emotional well-being of those we care about, demonstrating that we value and prioritize their feelings alongside our own.

## The Impact of Emotional Intelligence on Conflict Resolution

In the realm of conflict resolution, the power of emotional intelligence cannot be understated. It provides us with the tools to approach disagreements not as battlegrounds, but as opportunities for growth and understanding. Key components of emotional intelligence such as self-awareness, empathy, and effective communication skills are instrumental in de-escalating conflicts and paving the way toward amicable solutions.

When a disagreement arises, individuals equipped with emotional intelligence are able to remain calm and clear-headed, recognizing their own emotions and those of the other party without allowing them to cloud judgment. This self-awareness is critical for preventing the escalation of conflict and for facilitating a space where open, honest dialogue can flourish.

Empathy plays a pivotal role in conflict resolution by allowing us to understand the perspective and feelings of others, even when they differ from our own. This understanding fosters a sense of compassion and respect, making it easier to find common ground and work towards a resolution that acknowledges the needs and concerns of all parties involved.

Moreover, emotional intelligence enhances our communication skills, enabling us to express our thoughts and feelings in a way that is constructive rather than accusatory. It encourages active listening, a practice that ensures each person feels heard and validated, reducing defensiveness and opening up a pathway to mutual understanding.

In essence, emotional intelligence transforms the approach to conflict resolution, shifting the focus from winning an argument to solving a problem together. It's about recognizing the humanity in each other, even amidst disagreement, and striving for solutions that strengthen the relationship rather than erode it. By harnessing the principles of emotional intelligence, we can navigate conflicts with grace, leading to healthier, more resilient relationships.

# Building Mutual Respect and Understanding through EI

Emotional intelligence (EI) is a cornerstone of strong, resilient relationships, fostering an environment where mutual respect and understanding flourish. Cultivating EI enables us to approach interactions with a sense of empathy, allowing us to see beyond our perspectives and appreciate the feelings and thoughts of others. This shared empathy is the foundation upon which mutual respect is built. When both parties in a relationship can understand and honor their differences as well as their similarities, it creates a bond of trust that is both empowering and validating.

Effective communication is another critical aspect of building respect and understanding through EI. It involves more than just sharing our thoughts; it's about doing so with sensitivity and a genuine intention to understand the other person. This level of communication encourages openness, making it easier to navigate through misunderstandings and conflicts without damaging the relationship.

Additionally, recognizing and appreciating the emotional contributions of each person strengthens the connection. Acknowledging efforts made to maintain the relationship, expressing gratitude for the support received, and celebrating the successes of one another amplifies the sense of mutual respect. It sends a powerful message that each individual's feelings and needs are valued and important.

By integrating emotional intelligence into our daily interactions, we not only enhance our ability to relate to others but also contribute to a more supportive and understanding relationship dynamic. The practice of EI encourages us to be more mindful of our actions and words, leading to a more compassionate and respectful way of relating to one another. This approach not only enriches our personal relationships but also models positive emotional habits that can influence our broader social circles.

# The Journey of Developing Your Emotional Intelligence

Embarking on the path to bolster emotional intelligence is akin to setting off on a personal expedition, rich with self-discovery and opportunities for growth. This journey demands a steadfast commitment to introspection and the willingness to face one's emotional landscape with courage and openness. Central to this developmental process is the practice of self-reflection, a tool that allows us to delve into our thoughts, emotions, and reactions. By examining the roots of our feelings and behaviors, we can begin to understand the triggers that sway our emotional state and learn how to navigate them more effectively.

Engaging in continuous learning and seeking constructive feedback from those we trust are also pivotal steps in enhancing our emotional intelligence. Such interactions can provide invaluable insights into how our emotions and actions affect the people around us, offering a mirror to reflect on our interpersonal dynamics and areas for improvement. Likewise, embracing challenges and setbacks as learning opportunities rather than roadblocks can significantly accelerate our growth in emotional intelligence. These experiences, though often uncomfortable, are fertile ground for developing resilience, empathy, and better emotional regulation.

Additionally, practicing mindfulness and empathy towards oneself is crucial. This means acknowledging and accepting our emotions without harsh judgment, understanding that personal growth is a gradual process filled with peaks and valleys. As we navigate this journey, it's important to celebrate the small victories and progress we make along the way, understanding that each step forward brings us closer to becoming more emotionally intelligent and connected individuals. Through this continuous cycle of learning, reflecting, and applying, the development of our emotional intelligence becomes not just a goal but a rewarding journey of personal transformation.

## Real-Life Examples of Emotional Intelligence Transforming Relationships

The transformative power of emotional intelligence in relationships is vividly illustrated through numerous real-world examples. Consider the story of a married couple navigating the choppy waters of miscommunication. By implementing active listening techniques and striving to truly understand each other's emotional states, they managed to turn potential conflicts into moments of deep connection and mutual understanding. Their commitment to empathizing with each other's perspectives fostered a stronger, more resilient bond, illustrating how emotional intelligence can serve as a linchpin in marital harmony.

In another scenario, a longstanding friendship faced its toughest test when misunderstandings and unexpressed feelings led to a growing rift. However, by choosing to be vulnerable and openly sharing their fears and insecurities, the friends broke down the barriers that had formed between them. This act of courage and trust not only mended their relationship but also elevated it to a new level of intimacy and understanding.

Workplaces, too, benefit from the application of emotional intelligence. A team leader, recognizing the stress and burnout affecting her team, employed empathy and support to address their concerns. By acknowledging their emotions and offering practical solutions, she not only boosted morale but also cultivated a culture of mutual respect and collaboration that drove the team to greater success.

These examples underscore the profound impact emotional intelligence can have on our relationships. Whether in personal or professional spheres, the practice of emotional intelligence fosters an environment where trust, understanding, and connection thrive, transforming everyday interactions into meaningful, lasting bonds.

# CHAPTER 7: NAVIGATING THE SOCIAL LANDSCAPE WITH EMOTIONAL INTELLIGENCE AND COMMUNICATION

Communication is an essential skill in navigating the social landscape with emotional intelligence. One key aspect of effective communication is active listening. By practicing active listening, we can better understand others, build stronger relationships, and navigate social situations with greater ease.

## Understanding Active Listening

Active listening is more than just hearing the words that someone says; it's a comprehensive approach to communication that emphasizes full engagement with the speaker. This method requires the listener to immerse themselves in the conversation fully, employing not just their ears but also their mind and heart to process the information being shared. It's about creating a bridge of understanding between you and the speaker, facilitating a deeper connection and comprehension of the matter at hand.

At its core, active listening demands a high level of focus and concentration. It means tuning out external distractions and internal chatter, so the speaker feels valued and understood. This involves engaging with the content of what's being said, as well as the emotions and intentions behind the words. By doing so, listeners can capture the essence of the speaker's message, which often goes beyond the literal meaning of the words.

An integral part of active listening is the ability to recognize and respond to non-verbal cues. These cues, such as facial expressions, tone of voice, and body language, can provide significant insight into the speaker's true feelings and intentions. By paying attention to these subtle signals, listeners can gain a fuller understanding of what is being communicated, beyond the surface level.

The practice of active listening also necessitates a certain humility and willingness to put the speaker's needs at the forefront. It requires setting aside one's own thoughts and judgments temporarily to fully embrace another person's perspective. This doesn't mean you have to agree with everything that's said, but rather, it's about giving the speaker a platform to express themselves without fear of immediate criticism or dismissal.

By committing to active listening, individuals can foster a more meaningful and effective exchange of ideas. It's a skill that, when cultivated, not only enhances personal and professional relationships but also enriches the listener's understanding of the world around them.

## Preparing to Listen Actively

Entering a conversation with the right mindset is crucial for active listening. Preparation involves more than just being physically present; it requires a mental and emotional readiness to fully engage with another person's words and emotions. Begin by clearing your mind of distractions. This might mean putting away your phone, closing your laptop, or simply taking a moment to mentally shift your focus away from your own concerns and towards the speaker.

Acknowledging any biases or preconceptions you bring into the conversation is also key. We all carry our own views and experiences that shape how we interpret information, but being aware of these and setting them aside can open you up to truly hear what the speaker is saying. This openness is foundational in preventing misunderstandings and fostering genuine dialogue.

Next, commit to giving the speaker your undivided attention. This signals respect and shows the speaker they are valued, encouraging a more open and honest exchange. Position yourself to face the speaker, maintain eye contact, and adopt an open posture to non-verbally communicate your readiness to listen.

Emotionally, prepare yourself to be receptive and empathetic. This means being willing to understand the speaker's perspective, even if it differs from your own. Empathy does not require agreement but an appreciation for the speaker's feelings and viewpoints.

By mentally and emotionally preparing for a conversation, you not only set the stage for effective active listening but also demonstrate a commitment to understanding and engaging with the speaker on a deeper level. This preparation is a cornerstone of emotional intelligence in social interactions, facilitating a climate of respect and mutual understanding.

## The Four Key Components of Active Listening

The four key components of active listening are fundamental in enhancing communication and deepening connections. Firstly, paying attention to the speaker is paramount. This involves more than the passive reception of words; it requires an active engagement with the speaker's message, including the tone of voice, pace, and emotional undertones. This focus helps in absorbing the essence of what's being communicated.

Secondly, showing that you are listening is equally critical. This can be achieved through various non-verbal cues such as nodding, maintaining eye contact, and mirroring the speaker's expressions. These signals reassure the speaker of your engagement and interest in the conversation, fostering a more open and honest dialogue.

Thirdly, providing feedback is an integral aspect of active listening. This step involves reflecting on what has been said and offering thoughtful responses or questions. Feedback can take the form of paraphrasing the speaker's words to demonstrate understanding, or asking clarifying questions that encourage deeper exploration of the topic. This component underscores the listener's involvement and commitment to fully comprehending the speaker's perspective.

Finally, deferring judgment plays a crucial role in active listening. Suspending one's own opinions and refraining from immediate critique allows the listener to fully engage with the speaker's viewpoint. This openness is essential for a genuine exchange of ideas and promotes a safe environment for the speaker to share openly and honestly.

Incorporating these components into your listening habits can significantly enhance your ability to communicate effectively and navigate social interactions with empathy and understanding. Each element contributes to a more meaningful engagement, paving the way for richer, more fulfilling relationships.

## Techniques to Enhance Your Active Listening Skills

To elevate your active listening skills, several practical techniques can be implemented during conversations. One effective method is the use of reflective listening. This involves restating or summarizing what the speaker has said in your own words, which demonstrates that you have not only heard but also understood their message. Reflective listening encourages a deeper level of engagement and can often reveal any misunderstandings that need clarification.

Another technique is to encourage the speaker to continue sharing by using brief verbal affirmations like "I see," "Go on," or "Tell me more." These simple prompts show that you are interested and engaged without interrupting the speaker's flow of thought. They serve as gentle nudges that can help uncover more detailed insights or feelings the speaker may have.

Asking open-ended questions is also a key tactic in active listening. These are questions that cannot be answered with a simple yes or no. For example, asking, "How did that experience make you feel?" instead of "Did that make you upset?" encourages the speaker to open up more and share in greater depth. Open-ended questions promote richer conversations and demonstrate a genuine interest in understanding the speaker's perspective.

Lastly, managing your reactions is vital. It's important to maintain a neutral and open demeanor, avoiding quick judgments or jumping to conclusions. This can be challenging, especially when the topic is emotionally charged or when you have strong opinions. However, by focusing on the speaker and their needs in the moment, you can provide a safe space for honest and fruitful communication.

Implementing these techniques not only strengthens your active listening skills but also deepens your connections with others, fostering a sense of trust and mutual respect in your interactions.

## Common Barriers to Active Listening and How to Overcome Them

Active listening is an essential skill for effective communication, but several common barriers can hinder our ability to listen fully. These obstacles can significantly impact our social interactions and relationships. However, recognizing and addressing these barriers can greatly enhance our listening skills.

One major barrier is the presence of external distractions, such as background noise or visual stimuli. To combat this, choose a quiet, comfortable setting for conversations when possible, and minimize potential distractions beforehand. If in a noisy environment, focus intently on the speaker, perhaps by moving closer or positioning yourself to block out the noise.

Preconceived notions and personal biases are internal barriers that can distort our understanding of the speaker's message. To overcome these, consciously adopt an open-minded attitude toward each conversation. Remind yourself to set aside your judgments and listen with the intention of understanding the speaker's perspective, regardless of your initial impressions or beliefs.

A lack of interest in the topic or speaker can also prevent active listening. To address this, challenge yourself to find something valuable or intriguing in every conversation. Focusing on the emotional content or the speaker's passion about the topic can spark your interest and enhance your engagement.

Lastly, emotional reactions to sensitive topics can create a barrier to active listening. When discussing emotionally charged subjects, strive to maintain emotional equilibrium. Acknowledge your feelings but don't let them take over the conversation. This approach allows you to continue listening attentively and empathetically, even when the content is challenging.

By being mindful of these barriers and actively working to overcome them, you can improve your listening skills. This effort not only betters your communication but also deepens your connections with others, enriching your social interactions and relationships.

## Applying Active Listening in Different Contexts

Active listening is a versatile skill that transcends various settings, playing a critical role in enhancing understanding and rapport across different spheres of life. In personal relationships, it creates a foundation of trust and empathy, allowing individuals to express their thoughts and feelings without fear of judgment. This openness fosters deeper connections and a better understanding of each other's needs and perspectives.

In professional environments, active listening contributes to more effective teamwork and collaboration. It helps in accurately capturing instructions, feedback, and the nuances of team dynamics, leading to improved problem-solving and decision-making processes. By showing genuine interest and understanding in colleagues' viewpoints, a more inclusive and productive workplace culture is cultivated.

During social interactions, whether with acquaintances or strangers, active listening serves as a tool for building new relationships and networks. It enables one to navigate complex social nuances, identify common interests, and avoid misunderstandings. This skill is particularly valuable in cross-cultural situations, where differences in communication styles can easily lead to confusion or conflict. By actively listening, one demonstrates respect for diverse perspectives, facilitating smoother and more meaningful exchanges.

Furthermore, in conflict resolution scenarios, active listening can be a powerful mechanism for de-escalating tensions. By fully engaging with all parties' viewpoints without bias, it's possible to identify underlying issues and work towards a mutually satisfactory resolution.

In each of these contexts, the application of active listening fosters a sense of belonging and mutual respect, paving the way for more fulfilling and harmonious interactions. As such, mastering this skill is essential for anyone looking to navigate the complexities of human relationships with grace and emotional intelligence.

## Practice Makes Perfect: Ways to Sharpen Your Active Listening Skills

Improving your active listening skills is a journey of ongoing refinement and dedication. To cultivate this crucial ability, consider incorporating mindfulness exercises into your daily routine. Mindfulness helps in focusing your attention on the present moment, which is essential for active listening. It trains your mind to reduce distractions and increases your capacity to concentrate on the speaker's words and emotions.

Seeking feedback is another valuable strategy. After conversations, especially those you feel were significant or challenging, ask a trusted friend or colleague how well you listened. Were you fully engaged, or did your mind wander? Did you understand their main points? This feedback can provide insights into your listening habits and highlight areas for improvement.

Additionally, self-reflection plays a critical role in honing your active listening skills. Reflect on your recent interactions. Consider moments when you may have missed cues or responded inappropriately because you were formulating your response rather than truly listening. Use these reflections to set specific goals for improvement, such as minimizing interruptions or asking more open-ended questions in your next conversation.

Engaging in active listening exercises can also be beneficial. Practice with a partner by taking turns speaking and listening, then provide each other with feedback on the listening experience. This exercise can reveal surprising insights into how well you listen and show you direct paths for growth.

By deliberately practicing mindfulness, seeking and reflecting on feedback, and engaging in active listening exercises, you can steadily enhance your ability to listen actively. These efforts not only improve your listening skills but also deepen your connections with others, enriching both personal and professional relationships.

# CHAPTER 8: EMOTIONAL INTELLIGENCE: THE SECRET SAUCE OF EFFECTIVE LEADERSHIP

In the world of leadership, there is a secret sauce that sets apart the truly effective leaders from the rest. This secret sauce is known as emotional intelligence in leadership. Leaders who possess high emotional intelligence are able to navigate the complexities of human interactions with finesse, making them not just good leaders, but great ones. In this chapter, we will delve into the importance of emotional intelligence in leadership, exploring how it can transform teams, elevate spirits, enhance communication, and ultimately lead to a better workplace experience for everyone involved. Additionally, we will discuss the role of executive coaching in developing emotional intelligence among leaders.

## Understanding Emotional Intelligence in Leadership

At its core, emotional intelligence in leadership encapsulates the nuanced art of recognizing, understanding, and managing not only one's personal emotions but also those of the team one leads. This sophisticated skill set goes beyond mere emotional awareness; it's about leveraging that awareness to forge deeper connections, navigate the intricate social dynamics of the workplace, and catalyze collective action towards common goals.

In the realm of leadership, emotional intelligence serves as the linchpin for cultivating an environment where open dialogue, mutual respect, and understanding thrive. Leaders gifted with high emotional intelligence are adept at sensing the emotional undercurrents within their teams. They intuitively grasp how feelings can influence people's thoughts and behaviors and use this insight to guide their actions and decisions. It's this empathetic approach that allows them to address and defuse potential issues before they escalate, fostering a climate of stability and trust.

Moreover, emotional intelligence empowers leaders to provide feedback that resonates with their team members positively and constructively. Instead of delivering critiques or directives from a purely business standpoint, emotionally intelligent leaders tailor their communication to fit the individual's emotional state and personal motivators. This not only enhances the message's receptivity but also bolsters the individual's self-esteem and dedication to the team's objectives.

Another critical aspect of emotional intelligence in leadership is the capacity for self-regulation. Leaders who can manage their emotions and remain calm under pressure set a powerful example for their teams, demonstrating resilience and steadiness in the face of challenges. This ability to maintain emotional equilibrium not only helps in navigating crises but also in making thoughtful, informed decisions free from the cloud of immediate emotional reactions.

Emotional intelligence also extends to the leader's capacity to inspire and motivate. Understanding what makes each team member tick allows leaders to connect on a more personal level, tapping into their aspirations and anxieties. By aligning team goals with individual passions and concerns, leaders can kindle a shared sense of purpose and drive, propelling the team forward with a collective energy and focus.

In essence, emotional intelligence in leadership is about harmonizing the emotional and intellectual components of management. It's about leaders leveraging their emotional acuity to inspire trust, galvanize teams, and navigate the complex social landscape of the modern workplace with grace and efficacy. Through this lens, we begin to appreciate emotional intelligence not just as a beneficial trait but as an indispensable element of effective leadership.

# The Limitations of Technical Skills in Leadership

In the tapestry of leadership, technical skills are the threads that give form to a leader's vision, enabling them to navigate the tangible aspects of their role with expertise. However, these skills, while essential, are not sufficient in isolation for the intricate weave of effective leadership. The fabric of leadership is enriched by the interplay of emotional intelligence, without which, the texture of team dynamics, motivation, and collaboration becomes frayed.

Technical prowess can position a leader at the helm, but without emotional intelligence, they may find themselves steering the ship amidst a sea of disengaged crew members. The ability to crack complex codes or devise strategies can be rendered less impactful if a leader is unable to decode the emotional and relational aspects of their team. In the realm of leadership, it's not just about the what and the how, but significantly about the who and the why. Emotional intelligence is what bridges this gap, transforming transactions into interactions, and workforces into cohesive units.

A leader may have an encyclopedic knowledge of their industry and an impressive repertoire of technical skills, but this does not automatically equip them to inspire confidence, navigate conflicts sensitively, or foster an environment where creativity and innovation bloom. These are domains where emotional intelligence reigns supreme, serving as a catalyst for unlocking the full potential of a team. It's the difference between a leader who merely directs and one who truly connects and elevates those around them.

Technical skills enable a leader to understand the mechanics of their business, but emotional intelligence enables them to understand its heartbeat—the people. It's the people who drive innovation, who navigate through challenges, and who, when inspired, can achieve the extraordinary. Thus, the limitations of focusing solely on technical skills become evident in the diminished capacity to cultivate a vibrant, resilient, and dedicated workforce.

As the landscape of work continues to evolve, with increasing complexity and a greater emphasis on collaboration and adaptability, the reliance on technical skills alone is a narrow pathway. The broad avenue of leadership requires the complementary strengths of emotional intelligence to truly thrive, underscoring the fact that the essence of effective leadership transcends technical proficiency, embracing the rich, multifaceted spectrum of human emotion and connection.

## Emotional Intelligence as a Unifying Force in Teams

In the intricate dance of team dynamics, emotional intelligence serves as the rhythm that synchronizes individual movements into a cohesive performance. The essence of leadership involves not just steering the team toward its objectives but doing so in a way that each member feels seen, understood, and integral to the collective journey. This nuanced approach to leadership, grounded in emotional intelligence, acts as a potent unifying force within teams.

When leaders are attuned to their own emotional states and can adeptly navigate the emotional landscapes of their team members, a remarkable transformation occurs. This deep level of empathy and understanding cultivates an environment where open communication flourishes, and the fear of judgment or misunderstanding is significantly diminished. Team members are encouraged to share their ideas, concerns, and aspirations more freely, knowing that their contributions will be met with respect and consideration.

This open exchange of thoughts and feelings fosters a sense of belonging and commitment among team members. It's the difference between a group of individuals working next to each other and a unified team working with each other. Emotional intelligence in leadership bridges this gap, transforming the workplace into a setting where collaboration is not just a strategy but a shared value.

Moreover, leaders who harness emotional intelligence to unify their teams instill a collective resilience. Challenges and setbacks are inevitable in any endeavor, but a team bound by mutual understanding and shared purpose can navigate these hurdles more effectively. Instead of finger-pointing or disillusionment, setbacks become opportunities for growth and collective problem-solving. It's this resilient spirit, born from the unifying force of emotional intelligence, that propels teams toward excellence.

In practice, emotional intelligence manifests through the leader's ability to manage conflict with grace, recognize and celebrate individual contributions, and weave the diverse threads of their team into a strong tapestry. These actions are not just administrative duties but are heartfelt gestures that acknowledge the humanity at the core of every team.

The impact of emotional intelligence on team unity is profound. It is the catalyst that transforms mere groups of individuals into powerful, cohesive teams, united not just by common goals but by shared trust, respect, and understanding. In this way, emotional intelligence is indeed a unifying force, vital for any leader who aspires to not only achieve but inspire.

## Raising Spirits: The Role of Empathy and Understanding

Empathy and understanding stand as the twin pillars that uphold the edifice of emotional intelligence. These qualities imbue leaders with the profound ability to elevate the spirits of their team members, fostering an atmosphere where individuals do not just exist but thrive. In the labyrinth of leadership challenges, the ability to genuinely empathize and understand the unique perspectives and emotional landscapes of team members is akin to possessing a navigational compass, guiding leaders through the complexities of human emotions with grace and precision.

When leaders apply empathy in their interactions, they create a sanctuary for their team members—a space where vulnerabilities can be shared without fear of judgment. This empathetic engagement signals to team members that their feelings and experiences are not only recognized but valued. It's a subtle yet powerful form of validation that bolsters self-worth and nurtures a positive psychological state. Consequently, individuals feel more connected to their leader and the organization, nurturing a fertile ground for loyalty, dedication, and collective enthusiasm.

Understanding, the close kin of empathy, further enriches this dynamic. By striving to comprehend the motivations, fears, and aspirations of their team members, leaders can tailor their support and leadership strategies to align with the individual's needs and contexts. This bespoke approach to leadership acknowledges the individuality of team members, reinforcing their significance within the team and organization. It's an investment in the human capital that pays dividends in the form of enhanced morale and a vibrant, engaged workforce.

Moreover, in moments of adversity or challenge, empathy and understanding equip leaders with the sensitivity to offer not just solutions but solace. They become adept at not only addressing the issue at hand but also in healing the emotional fallout that may accompany such challenges. It's this capacity to uplift spirits and provide a steadying presence that can transform a moment of difficulty into an opportunity for growth and deeper connection within the team.

Empathy and understanding, therefore, are not mere soft skills in the arsenal of a leader; they are the essence of a leadership philosophy that cherishes and elevates the human spirit. In cultivating these qualities, leaders not only raise the spirits of their teams but also pave the way for a more cohesive, resilient, and joyful journey towards collective goals.

## Enhancing Communication Through Emotional Intelligence

In the tapestry of leadership skills, the ability to communicate effectively is paramount. Emotional intelligence elevates this ability, transforming basic exchanges into deeply impactful dialogues. Leaders who harness emotional intelligence navigate the subtleties of human emotion with precision, ensuring their messages not only reach their intended audience but resonate on a profound level.

This nuanced approach to communication begins with active listening—an aspect significantly enriched by emotional intelligence. Leaders adept in this realm tune into more than just the words spoken; they are sensitive to the nuances of tone, body language, and unspoken sentiments. This heightened level of attentiveness allows leaders to respond not merely to the surface content of a conversation but to the deeper emotional currents flowing beneath. Such responses demonstrate a genuine understanding and respect for team members 'perspectives, fostering a sense of being truly heard and valued.

Moreover, emotional intelligence guides leaders in the art of timing and delivery. They become attuned to the emotional readiness of their team members to receive feedback, whether positive or constructive. This sensitivity ensures that messages are delivered in a manner that encourages receptivity, growth, and positive action, rather than defensiveness or disengagement. It's a skill that turns potential conflict into opportunities for strengthening trust and rapport.

In addition, emotionally intelligent leaders excel in adapting their communication style to suit the diverse personalities within their teams. They recognize that a one-size-fits-all approach falls short in addressing the unique motivational drivers and emotional needs of individuals. By customizing their interaction style, leaders can more effectively engage, inspire, and mobilize their teams toward shared goals.

This mastery of emotional intelligence in communication also extends to non-verbal cues. Leaders aware of their own body language—and how it's perceived—can ensure their non-verbal signals align with their intended message, reinforcing trust and clarity in their interactions.

Through emotional intelligence, communication transcends the mere exchange of information. It becomes a powerful tool for building connections, aligning visions, and nurturing an environment where every voice is heard and valued. In this way, leaders do not just speak; they resonate, leaving a lasting imprint on the hearts and minds of their team members.

## The Impact of Emotional Intelligence on Workplace Culture

The influence of a leader's emotional intelligence on the fabric of workplace culture cannot be overstated. When leaders prioritize understanding, empathy, and effective communication—hallmarks of high emotional intelligence—they lay the foundation for a culture that thrives on openness and trust. This transformative leadership approach encourages an environment where team members feel valued and understood, leading to deeper connections and a stronger sense of community within the workplace.

A culture infused with emotional intelligence is characterized by its resilience, adaptability, and collaborative spirit. Challenges are met with collective problem-solving rather than finger-pointing, and failures are seen as opportunities for growth rather than grounds for blame. This positive atmosphere nurtures a sense of security among employees, empowering them to take creative risks and innovate without fear of judgment or failure.

Furthermore, emotional intelligence in leadership promotes inclusivity and diversity by recognizing and valuing the unique contributions of each team member. This acknowledgment not only enhances individual self-esteem but also enriches the collective intelligence of the team. By fostering an environment where diverse perspectives are celebrated, leaders can unlock a wealth of creative solutions and strategies that might otherwise remain untapped.

Leaders who exemplify emotional intelligence also demonstrate a commitment to personal and professional growth, both for themselves and their teams. This commitment to continuous learning and development signals to employees that their growth is a priority, contributing to a culture of lifelong learning. As team members feel supported in their developmental journeys, their loyalty and commitment to the organization deepen, reducing turnover and building a stable, experienced workforce.

By embedding emotional intelligence into the very fabric of workplace culture, leaders not only enhance the day-to-day experience of their teams but also set the stage for sustained organizational success. This culture of emotional intelligence cultivates a workplace where respect, understanding, and mutual support are not just ideals but lived realities, driving the organization forward with a shared sense of purpose and passion.

## Emotional Intelligence and Profitability: Connecting the Dots

At first glance, the link between emotional intelligence and profitability might not seem obvious. However, delve a bit deeper, and the connection becomes unmistakably clear. Leaders who navigate the complexities of their roles with a high degree of emotional intelligence foster environments ripe for success, underpinning the very fabric of their organizations with the qualities necessary for financial prosperity.

The relationship between emotional intelligence in leadership and an organization's bottom line is multifaceted. For starters, emotionally intelligent leaders are masters at cultivating a workplace culture that prizes engagement, dedication, and a strong sense of belonging. Employees who feel understood, valued, and emotionally connected to their workplace are not just happier but also significantly more productive. This heightened productivity directly translates into better performance, innovation, and, ultimately, enhanced profitability.

Moreover, emotionally intelligent leadership directly correlates with lower turnover rates. The costs associated with replacing an employee can be substantial, not just in direct expenses but also in the loss of institutional knowledge, decreased morale, and the ripple effects on team productivity. By creating an environment where employees feel genuinely appreciated and aligned with the organization's goals, leaders can significantly reduce turnover, thereby safeguarding the organization's financial health and stability.

Additionally, the adept conflict resolution and problem-solving capabilities of emotionally intelligent leaders minimize disruptions and keep teams focused and efficient. This efficiency is crucial for maintaining a competitive edge and driving continuous improvement in products, services, and processes—all key contributors to an organization's profitability.

Finally, in today's global market, the ability to navigate diverse cultural and emotional landscapes is invaluable. Leaders with high emotional intelligence are better equipped to understand and meet the needs of a diverse clientele, adapt to global market trends, and lead cross-cultural teams, further contributing to an organization's profitability through expanded market reach and innovation.

In essence, the pathway from emotional intelligence in leadership to profitability is paved with the enhanced performance, engagement, and efficiency that emotionally intelligent leaders foster. By recognizing and harnessing the profound impact of emotional intelligence on the financial success of their organizations, leaders can unlock new levels of achievement and sustainability in the ever-evolving landscape of business.

# Developing Emotional Intelligence Through Executive Coaching

The journey to elevating one's emotional intelligence, particularly for those in leadership positions, is both intricate and deeply personal. Executive coaching emerges as a pivotal element in this transformative process, offering a tailored pathway to mastering the art of emotional agility. This bespoke development experience is more than a mere enhancement of leadership skills; it's an exploration into the very fabric of a leader's interpersonal dynamics, emotional regulation, and empathy.

A core aspect of executive coaching lies in its ability to mirror back to leaders their emotional patterns, blind spots, and strengths in a way that self-reflection alone might not reveal. Through targeted conversations and exercises, coaches work closely with leaders to unpack the layers of their emotional intelligence, pinpointing areas for growth such as empathetic listening, emotional self-awareness, and the nuanced management of team dynamics. It's this guided introspection and skill-building that fosters a profound shift in how leaders perceive and engage with their emotions and those of others.

Moreover, executive coaching offers a safe space for leaders to experiment with and refine new strategies for emotional engagement, conflict resolution, and motivational leadership. This hands-on approach ensures that the principles of emotional intelligence are not just understood but are ingrained and practiced in real-world scenarios. The result is a leader who not only excels in the cognitive aspects of their role but thrives in the emotional dimensions of leadership, enhancing team cohesion, employee satisfaction, and ultimately, organizational success.

The ripple effect of such development is significant. As leaders become more emotionally intelligent, they set in motion a cultural shift within their organizations, promoting an ethos of emotional awareness, open communication, and mutual respect. This cultural transformation is instrumental in navigating the complexities of today's business landscape, marked by rapid change and diverse workforces.

In essence, executive coaching serves as a catalyst for unlocking the full potential of emotional intelligence in leadership. It's an investment in the human element of leadership, which, in turn, reaps dividends in organizational harmony, resilience, and performance. Through this focused development journey, leaders are not just equipped to lead with authority but with empathy, understanding, and a profound connection to their teams and the broader organizational mission.

# CHAPTER 9: EMOTIONAL INTELLIGENCE: THE KEY TO SUCCESS IN EVERY SPHERE OF LIFE

In today's fast-paced and competitive world, emotional intelligence is a crucial skill that can make all the difference in one's personal and professional success. Whether you are in the workplace, educational setting, or even focusing on your mental health, emotional intelligence is a valuable tool that is useful wherever you are.

## The Foundation of Emotional Intelligence

At its core, emotional intelligence is the art and science of harnessing our emotions to foster better understanding, both of ourselves and those around us. It's about delving deep into our emotional repertoire, recognizing the nuances of our feelings, and using this insight to guide our thoughts and actions in a direction that benefits both our personal and professional lives. This profound ability enables us to see beyond the surface of mere reactions, to the underlying emotions that drive those reactions.

Emotional intelligence is built upon four key pillars: self-awareness, self-management, social awareness, and relationship management. Self-awareness involves having a clear understanding of our emotions, strengths, weaknesses, and drives. It's about recognizing how our emotions affect our thoughts and behaviors and knowing how others perceive us. Self-management, on the other hand, focuses on our ability to regulate and control our emotions, especially in stressful situations or when faced with adversity. It's about staying in control, exhibiting flexibility, and maintaining a positive attitude.

Social awareness is the ability to accurately pick up on emotions in other people and understand what is really going on with them. This includes empathy, the capacity to grasp the emotions of others without their explicit communication. Finally, relationship management involves using our awareness of our own emotions and those of others to navigate interactions successfully. This includes clear communication, effective handling of conflict, and inspiring and influencing others in a positive way.

The mastery of these components of emotional intelligence empowers individuals to navigate the complex social environments of the workplace, educational settings, and personal relationships with grace and efficiency. It allows for a deeper connection with others, fostering environments where creativity and productivity thrive. Emotional intelligence is not static; it's a set of skills that we can all develop and improve over time with practice and intentionality.

Understanding and developing emotional intelligence requires a commitment to self-reflection and an openness to feedback from others. It involves pausing to consider our emotional responses rather than reacting impulsively. It means listening closely to what others are communicating, both verbally and non-verbally, and responding in a way that is empathetic and constructive.

In essence, emotional intelligence serves as the foundation for a myriad of positive outcomes in our lives. From improving our relationships and making sound decisions to managing stress and inspiring those around us, the benefits of developing a high level of emotional intelligence are profound and far-reaching. By cultivating these skills, we not only enhance our own well-being but also contribute to a more understanding, empathetic, and productive world.

## Navigating Workplace Challenges with Emotional Intelligence

In the intricate labyrinth of the modern workplace, emotional intelligence emerges as a beacon of guidance, facilitating the smooth navigation of the myriad challenges that professionals face daily. It transcends the mere ability to work well under pressure, embodying the capacity to foster a climate of mutual respect, understanding, and collaboration among colleagues. The essence of emotional intelligence in the workplace lies not only in self-regulation and personal resilience but also in its power to enhance team dynamics, catalyze innovation, and streamline conflict resolution.

The workplace, with its diverse personalities and constant demands, often tests our emotional limits. Emotional intelligence equips individuals with the ability to recognize these stressors not as insurmountable barriers but as opportunities for growth and learning. This perspective shift is crucial in managing stress and preventing the all-too-common phenomenon of burnout. By understanding our emotional triggers and developing strategies to address them proactively, we cultivate a resilience that sustains our passion and productivity, even when the going gets tough.

Moreover, emotional intelligence plays a pivotal role in enhancing team dynamics. It's about more than just getting along with coworkers; it's about deeply understanding their viewpoints, motivations, and emotions. This level of empathy allows for the creation of a supportive work environment where everyone feels valued and understood. In such a climate, collaboration flourishes, and with it, the innovative solutions and breakthroughs that propel organizations forward. The ability to navigate interpersonal relationships with finesse and empathy leads to stronger, more cohesive teams that are adept at tackling complex challenges together.

Conflict is an inevitable aspect of any workplace, yet it's the approach to conflict that distinguishes successful teams. Emotional intelligence is a critical tool in this regard, offering strategies for constructive conflict resolution. It involves actively listening to differing opinions, validating emotions, and collaboratively finding solutions that respect all parties' needs. This approach not only resolves the immediate issue but also strengthens trust and respect among team members, laying the groundwork for more effective collaboration in the future.

Emotional intelligence also extends its benefits to leadership, transforming the way leaders connect with, inspire, and guide their teams. A leader with high emotional intelligence is adept at recognizing the unique strengths and needs of their team members, adapting their leadership style to suit these variables. This personalized approach fosters an environment where employees feel genuinely seen and supported, increasing their engagement and loyalty to the organization. Leaders who model emotional intelligence set a powerful example, encouraging a workplace culture where empathy, mutual respect, and open communication are the norms rather than the exceptions.

In the ever-evolving landscape of the workplace, emotional intelligence stands out as a key differentiator for individuals and organizations alike. It's a multifaceted tool that, when wielded with skill and sensitivity, can transform challenges into opportunities for growth, innovation, and collaboration. By prioritizing the development of emotional intelligence, both at an individual and organizational level, we pave the way for not only enhanced productivity and success but also for workplaces that are more humane, compassionate, and resilient.

## The Role of Emotional Intelligence in Education

Emotional intelligence stands as a pivotal pillar within the educational sphere, shaping not only academic success but also the overall well-being of students. In an environment as dynamic and diverse as a classroom, the ability to navigate emotions effectively becomes a critical skill for both educators and students alike.

Educators, equipped with an understanding of emotional intelligence, are better positioned to create a learning environment that is not only intellectually stimulating but also emotionally supportive. By integrating emotional intelligence into their teaching methods, educators can engage students in a manner that transcends traditional academic learning. It involves recognizing the emotional states of students, understanding their individual needs, and adapting teaching strategies to meet these needs. This tailored approach ensures that learning becomes a more inclusive, personal, and ultimately more effective process.

For students, the development of emotional intelligence is transformative. It lays the foundation for essential skills such as empathy, resilience, and self-regulation. In the classroom, students who are emotionally intelligent are more adept at handling stress, overcoming challenges, and staying motivated. They can better manage their emotions during exams, presentations, and group projects, which are often sources of significant stress. Additionally, these students exhibit a heightened ability to communicate with peers and educators, fostering a more collaborative and supportive learning environment.

Beyond the immediate classroom benefits, fostering emotional intelligence in students prepares them for the complexities of the wider world. It equips them with the skills to navigate interpersonal relationships, pursue lifelong learning, and enter the workforce as emotionally competent individuals. In essence, the cultivation of emotional intelligence in education is not merely about academic achievement; it's about preparing students to lead fulfilling lives.

Furthermore, the role of emotional intelligence in education extends to conflict resolution and the promotion of a positive school culture. Students with high emotional intelligence are more likely to understand the perspectives of others and engage in constructive dialogue. This capability is invaluable in resolving conflicts amicably and building a school environment rooted in mutual respect and understanding.

Emotional intelligence in education also plays a crucial role in the development of leadership skills among students. It empowers them to take on leadership roles with confidence, guiding their peers with empathy, and making decisions that consider the well-being of all involved. These leadership experiences, nurtured in an educational setting, lay the groundwork for future leaders who are as emotionally intelligent as they are academically knowledgeable.

In the quest to educate the whole student, emotional intelligence emerges not as an optional add-on but as a core component of a holistic education. The integration of emotional intelligence into the curriculum signifies a shift towards education that values emotional well-being as much as academic excellence. By championing emotional intelligence, educators can inspire a generation of students who are not only smart but also emotionally astute, resilient, and empathetic—qualities that are indispensable in both personal and professional realms.

In this way, the role of emotional intelligence in education transcends the boundaries of the classroom, influencing every aspect of a student's life. It's about nurturing hearts as well as minds, preparing students not just for tests, but for the tests of life. Through the deliberate development of emotional intelligence, the educational experience becomes a transformative journey, shaping students into well-rounded individuals ready to contribute positively to society.

## Strengthening Mental Health through Emotional Intelligence

Navigating the complexities of mental health requires a multifaceted approach, and central to this journey is the role of emotional intelligence. The ability to adeptly understand, utilize, and manage our emotions serves as a cornerstone for building resilience against the mental challenges that life throws our way. Far from being just an ancillary skill, emotional intelligence is deeply intertwined with our psychological well-being, offering a buffer against the vicissitudes of mental health struggles.

At the heart of emotional intelligence lies the capacity for self-regulation—a skill paramount in coping with stress and anxiety. The practice of self-regulation allows us to step back from our immediate, often impulsive reactions to stressors, providing the space to respond in a more measured and effective manner. This conscious navigation and management of our emotions equip us with a robust toolkit to mitigate the impacts of stress, potentially averting the descent into chronic anxiety or depression.

Moreover, emotional intelligence fosters a nuanced understanding of our emotional landscape. By cultivating a deep awareness of our feelings, we open the door to recognizing early warning signs of mental distress. This proactive identification is critical, as it enables timely intervention and support, thereby preventing the exacerbation of mental health issues. The introspective aspect of emotional intelligence not only aids in our self-care but also enhances our empathy towards others who may be experiencing similar challenges.

Empathy, a fundamental component of emotional intelligence, extends its benefits beyond self-understanding to encompass the realm of interpersonal relationships. A high degree of empathy encourages a supportive and understanding approach to interactions with others, fostering a sense of connectedness and social support. These social bonds are instrumental in safeguarding mental health, as they provide a network of care that can offer encouragement and understanding during difficult times. The capacity to empathize and connect deeply with others also allows for more meaningful and fulfilling relationships, which are essential for emotional well-being.

The implications of emotional intelligence for mental health are profound when considering its role in emotion-focused coping strategies. By leveraging our understanding of emotions, we can select coping mechanisms that directly address our emotional needs, rather than resorting to avoidance or denial. Such strategies might include seeking social support, engaging in self-reflection, or practicing mindfulness—each rooted in the principles of emotional intelligence.

Additionally, emotional intelligence equips us with the ability to maintain a positive outlook even in the face of adversity. The skillful management of emotions contributes to a more optimistic and resilient mindset, which is pivotal in overcoming challenges and recovering from setbacks. This optimistic resilience not only enhances our ability to navigate personal trials but also inspires a similar strength in those around us, creating a more resilient community.

In the intricate dance of mental health, emotional intelligence emerges as a vital partner, guiding us through both our internal struggles and our interactions with the world. By embracing and cultivating these emotional skills, we arm ourselves with the necessary tools to protect our mental well-being, ensuring that we can face life's challenges with strength, grace, and resilience.

# The Impact of Emotional Intelligence on Leadership

In the realm of leadership, emotional intelligence emerges as an indispensable asset, transforming the way leaders connect with, guide, and inspire their teams. A leader endowed with high emotional intelligence possesses a keen ability to perceive, understand, and manage not only their own emotions but those of their team members as well. This profound skill set allows them to foster a workplace environment that is both positive and inclusive, cultivating a sense of belonging and motivation among employees.

The hallmark of an emotionally intelligent leader is their capacity for empathy. This goes beyond mere understanding; it involves a deep and genuine concern for team members' well-being and professional growth. By empathetically engaging with their teams, leaders are able to build strong, trust-based relationships that serve as the foundation for team cohesion and cooperation. These relationships are critical for facilitating open communication, ensuring that team members feel heard, valued, and understood.

Moreover, emotionally intelligent leaders are adept at recognizing the diverse emotional needs and strengths of their team members. They can tailor their leadership style to meet these needs, thereby maximizing each individual's potential. This personalized approach not only enhances job satisfaction and performance but also contributes to the personal development of team members, empowering them to take on new challenges and responsibilities with confidence.

Conflict resolution is another area where emotional intelligence proves invaluable for leaders. By approaching conflicts with a mindset focused on finding mutually beneficial solutions, leaders can navigate disagreements with tact and diplomacy. They understand that acknowledging and addressing the emotions at play in conflicts is key to resolving them in a way that strengthens team bonds rather than weakening them. This ability to turn potential discord into an opportunity for growth and understanding is a testament to the transformative power of emotional intelligence in leadership.

The influence of an emotionally intelligent leader extends beyond the immediate team to shape the broader organizational culture. Leaders who exemplify emotional intelligence set a standard for behavior that encourages empathy, respect, and collaboration throughout the organization. This creates a ripple effect, fostering a culture where employees at all levels feel motivated to develop their own emotional intelligence skills. As a result, the entire organization becomes more agile, resilient, and better equipped to face challenges.

Furthermore, emotionally intelligent leaders are champions of innovation. They understand that a climate of psychological safety — where team members feel safe to express ideas, take risks, and admit mistakes — is essential for creativity and innovation. By cultivating such an environment, leaders not only spur innovation but also contribute to a learning culture where continuous improvement is the norm.

In leadership, the impact of emotional intelligence is profound and multifaceted. It transforms leaders into more effective, empathetic, and inspiring figures who are capable of bringing out the best in their teams. Such leaders are not only adept at navigating the complex dynamics of the workplace but also at steering their organizations toward sustained success and growth. The development and refinement of emotional intelligence skills in leadership are, therefore, not just advantageous but essential in today's rapidly changing business landscape.

## Building Personal Relationships through Emotional Intelligence

Emotional intelligence shines as a beacon in the landscape of personal relationships, serving as a cornerstone for developing deep, meaningful connections. This facet of our skill set, emphasizing understanding and managing emotions, enables us to navigate the intricate nuances of personal interactions with grace and empathy. It is through this lens of emotional intelligence that we are able to forge bonds that are not only strong but also nurturing and fulfilling.

Effective communication is the bedrock upon which emotional intelligence in personal relationships is built. It transcends the mere exchange of words, encompassing the ability to convey feelings and understandings without misunderstanding. By actively listening and expressing ourselves with clarity and consideration, we pave the way for open and honest dialogue. This level of communication fosters a sense of security and trust, essential ingredients for any thriving relationship.

Empathy plays a pivotal role in emotional intelligence, particularly in personal contexts. It is the ability to step into the shoes of another, to feel what they feel, and see the world from their perspective. This profound understanding allows us to connect on a deeper level, validating the emotions of those we care about and offering support that is genuinely attuned to their needs. Empathy is the glue that binds, enabling us to navigate the ups and downs of relationships with compassion and sensitivity.

Conflict, while often viewed negatively, is an inevitable aspect of close relationships. However, it is the approach to conflict resolution that determines the health and longevity of a relationship. Emotional intelligence equips us with the tools to handle disagreements constructively, without resorting to hurtful behaviors or words. It encourages us to approach conflicts with a problem-solving mindset, seeking solutions that acknowledge and respect everyone's feelings and needs.

This approach not only resolves the immediate issue but also strengthens the relationship, building resilience against future challenges.

Moreover, emotional intelligence fosters an environment of mutual growth and support. It encourages us to celebrate the successes of our loved ones and to stand by them during times of struggle. By sharing in the joys and sorrows of those we care about, we deepen our connections and create a shared history that enriches our relationship.

The journey of building and maintaining strong personal relationships through emotional intelligence is ongoing. It requires a commitment to self-improvement and a willingness to learn from each interaction. It involves checking in with our emotions, recognizing when they may be influencing our behavior in unhelpful ways, and taking steps to address this. By continually practicing the principles of emotional intelligence, we not only enhance our own lives but also contribute to the well-being and happiness of those around us.

In essence, emotional intelligence is more than a tool for personal success; it is a gift we offer to those we love. It allows us to be fully present in our relationships, to love deeply, and to navigate the complexities of human emotions with grace. Through the cultivation of emotional intelligence, we unlock the potential for relationships that are rich, rewarding, and resilient, standing the test of time.

# CHAPTER 10: BRIDGING THE GAP: EMOTIONAL INTELLIGENCE IN ARTIFICIAL INTELLIGENCE

In today's rapidly advancing technological landscape, the intersection of emotional intelligence and artificial intelligence has become increasingly crucial. As we delve into the realm of AI development, understanding human emotions plays a pivotal role in shaping the future of technology. The synergy between emotional intelligence and artificial intelligence opens up a myriad of possibilities for creating more empathetic and intuitive systems that can revolutionize the way we interact with machines. Let's explore how emotional intelligence is bridging the gap in artificial intelligence.

## Understanding Emotional Intelligence and Its Components

At its core, emotional intelligence is a nuanced blend of capabilities that enable an individual to navigate the complexities of emotional landscapes, both within oneself and in interactions with others. This multifaceted skill set encompasses several critical components, each contributing to how effectively we perceive, connect with, and influence the emotional states around us.

The first of these components is self-awareness. This is the ability to recognize and understand one's own emotions, pinpointing their origins and recognizing their impact on thoughts and actions. It's like having an internal mirror, reflecting back on our emotional state with clarity and honesty.

Next, we delve into self-regulation, which is essentially about managing those emotions. This doesn't mean suppressing feelings but rather understanding them well enough to respond in ways that are measured and consistent with one's values. Imagine being in the eye of an emotional storm but still being able to steer the ship with steady hands; that's self-regulation.

Empathy, another cornerstone of emotional intelligence, extends our understanding beyond our personal emotions to the feelings of others. It's the bridge that connects us, allowing us to perceive and appreciate the emotions of those around us, fostering a sense of compassion and understanding.

Lastly, effective social skills enable us to use our emotional awareness and empathy to navigate social complexities, build positive relationships, and influence others. It's the toolkit for interacting in a way that is both responsive and constructive, enhancing our ability to communicate, collaborate, and resolve conflicts.

Integrating these components of emotional intelligence into artificial intelligence represents a formidable challenge but one that holds the promise of creating AI systems that are not only intelligent but also possess a kind of emotional acumen. The goal is to craft technology that understands and interacts with us on a fundamentally human level, transforming our relationship with machines into something more akin to a genuine human connection.

## The Evolution of Artificial Intelligence: From Logic to Emotion

The journey of artificial intelligence from a purely logical framework to an emotionally intelligent partner mirrors the evolution of human understanding itself. Initially, AI's capabilities were confined to binary decisions, mathematical calculations, and executing commands without understanding the nuances of human emotion or social subtleties. These systems operated in a world of clear-cut logic, where answers were right or wrong with no shades of grey in between.

As the digital age accelerates, the narrative for AI has shifted significantly. The focus is no longer solely on creating systems that excel in logic and computation but on developing AI that understands and processes the complexity of human emotions. This monumental shift acknowledges that for technology to be genuinely interactive and immersive, it must go beyond cold calculations to embrace the warmth of human feelings.

The essence of this evolution lies in recognizing that emotional intelligence is as critical to decision-making as logical reasoning. When humans make decisions, they don't rely purely on logic; emotions play a crucial role. Therefore, infusing AI with emotional intelligence means teaching machines not just to think but to feel—or at least mimic the process of feeling in a way that reflects human experiences. This involves interpreting verbal cues, facial expressions, and body language to gauge emotions and react in a manner that a human would perceive as understanding and empathetic.

To achieve this, developers and researchers are harnessing vast datasets of emotional responses, utilizing machine learning algorithms to detect and interpret the subtleties of human emotion. This not just enhances the user experience but fundamentally alters the interaction paradigm between humans and machines. The AI of the future, enriched with emotional intelligence, promises to be more than just a tool; it aims to be a companion that understands us, perhaps sometimes better than we understand ourselves.

This transformative journey from logic to emotion in AI underscores a broader narrative of technological advancement—one that strives to make machines more like us, not just in intelligence but in empathy and understanding. This endeavor goes beyond technical innovation; it is about enriching the human experience, making our interactions with technology more natural, intuitive, and, ultimately, more meaningful.

## The Significance of Emotion in Human-AI Interaction

In the tapestry of human interactions, emotions serve as the threads that bind our communications and relationships, imbuing them with depth and meaning. The endeavor to weave these threads into the fabric of artificial intelligence is more than a technological ambition; it's a step towards creating a world where machines don't just understand our commands but our sentiments as well. By infusing AI with emotional intelligence, we unlock a realm of possibilities where interactions with technology are enriched by empathy and understanding, fundamentally enhancing the user experience.

The significance of emotion in human-AI interaction cannot be overstated. It's about transforming transactions into interactions, and exchanges into connections. When AI systems can perceive and process our emotions, they can respond in ways that are not only relevant but also resonate on a human level. This capacity for emotionally intelligent responses can revolutionize customer service, making experiences feel less like dealing with a machine and more like engaging with a human who understands your feelings and can adapt to them. It's the difference between a robotic, "How can I assist you today?" and an intuitive, "I can see this is important to you; let's figure it out together."

In educational settings, emotionally intelligent AI can provide students with tailored support, recognizing frustration or confusion and adapting its teaching methods accordingly. In health care, it can offer comfort, understanding, and assistance in ways that are sensitive to the patient's emotional state. Across every sector, the integration of emotional intelligence into AI has the potential to make technology feel less like an interloper in the human world and more like a natural extension of our social fabric.

However, as we navigate this promising frontier, it is crucial to approach with both enthusiasm and caution. Ensuring that these emotionally intelligent systems are designed with ethical considerations and human values at their core is paramount. As we teach machines to understand and engage with our emotions, we must also imbue them with the principles of respect, privacy, and empathy. In doing so, we not only enhance the user experience but also safeguard our human dignity.

# Emotional Recognition Technologies: Paving the Way

In the vanguard of the fusion between emotional intelligence and artificial intelligence stand the advancements in emotional recognition technologies. These sophisticated tools are the keystones that allow AI to delve beyond the surface, interpreting the rich tapestry of human emotions through facial expressions, voice nuances, and subtle body language cues. It is through these technologies that AI begins to grasp the silent language of our emotions, turning what was once a complex puzzle into an understandable narrative.

Emotional recognition technologies serve as a bridge, enabling AI systems to cross from mere data processors to entities capable of engaging with the emotional fabric of human experience. By analyzing the intricate patterns of our expressions and the tonal variations in our speech, these technologies equip AI with the ability to perceive and, to some extent, understand the emotional currents flowing through human interactions. This capability marks a pivotal shift in the development of AI, transforming it into a more relatable and empathetic presence in our lives.

The implications of this technological leap are profound. With emotional recognition capabilities, AI systems can adapt their responses to align with the emotional context of a situation, offering support that feels both timely and attuned to our needs. Imagine a virtual assistant that can detect stress in your voice and respond in a soothing tone, or an educational program that recognizes confusion on a student's face and automatically adjusts its teaching method to be more supportive. These scenarios, once relegated to the realm of science fiction, are increasingly within the realm of possibility.

However, the path forward is not without its hurdles. The precision of emotional recognition technologies, while impressive, continues to evolve. The challenge lies not only in refining the accuracy of these systems but also in navigating the ethical terrain they inhabit. As these technologies become more embedded in our daily lives, questions of privacy, consent, and emotional authenticity come to the fore, reminding us that the journey toward emotionally intelligent AI is as much about technological innovation as it is about ethical responsibility.

## Challenges in Merging Emotional and Artificial Intelligence

As we navigate the convergence of emotional and artificial intelligence, the journey is marked by a terrain of complexities that challenges both our technological prowess and our ethical compass. The endeavor to meld these two realms introduces a series of hurdles that are as intricate as the human emotions we seek to understand.

One of the primary challenges lies in the realm of data privacy and the ethical handling of sensitive emotional information. As AI systems become more adept at interpreting human emotions, they require access to vast amounts of personal data, raising significant concerns about privacy and the potential for misuse. Ensuring that these systems respect individual privacy rights while still providing meaningful emotional insights necessitates a delicate balance, one that hinges on robust data protection measures and transparent data handling practices.

Moreover, the specter of bias in emotional recognition technologies looms large. The data sets used to train these systems often reflect the implicit biases of those who create them, potentially leading to AI that misinterprets or misrepresents the emotional states of individuals from diverse backgrounds. Addressing this challenge requires a concerted effort to cultivate diverse data sets and implement algorithms that can discern and mitigate these biases, ensuring that emotionally intelligent AI is inclusive and equitable.

Another critical hurdle is the ethical use of emotionally intelligent AI. As these systems gain the capability to understand and influence human emotions, the potential for manipulation or coercion arises. This calls for the establishment of ethical guidelines that govern the development and application of emotionally intelligent AI, ensuring that these technologies are used in ways that are beneficial and non-exploitative.

Navigating these challenges is paramount to the successful integration of emotional intelligence into artificial intelligence. It demands a multidisciplinary approach that combines technological innovation with ethical foresight, ensuring that as we forge ahead, we do so with a commitment to advancing technology that respects our humanity and enriches our emotional well-being.

## Ethical Implications of Emotionally Intelligent AI

As we forge deeper into the era of emotionally intelligent AI, we encounter a complex web of ethical considerations that demands our attention. The core of these ethical debates centers on how we navigate the intersection of human emotions and artificial intelligence with integrity and responsibility. The advent of emotionally intelligent AI introduces profound questions regarding how emotional data is collected, analyzed, and utilized, laying bare the necessity for stringent ethical standards and rigorous oversight.

Central to the ethical discourse is the imperative to protect individual privacy. The very essence of emotionally intelligent AI hinges on its ability to discern and interact with human emotions, a process that inherently involves access to sensitive personal information. The challenge lies in implementing systems that can leverage this data for positive outcomes, such as enhancing user experience and fostering emotional well-being, while staunchly guarding against any breach of privacy. This delicate balance calls for encryption methods and data protection protocols that are both robust and transparent, ensuring that users' emotional landscapes are navigated with the utmost respect and confidentiality.

Moreover, the issue of consent emerges as a critical ethical pillar. Users must be fully informed about how their emotional data will be used and must retain control over this information. This involves clear, understandable consent processes that empower users to make informed decisions about their participation in emotionally intelligent AI systems.

Transparency, too, plays a vital role in the ethical framework surrounding emotionally intelligent AI. Stakeholders, from developers to end-users, should have a clear understanding of how these systems operate, the nature of the data they collect, and the mechanisms in place to protect this data. This transparency is essential not only for building trust but also for fostering an environment where ethical considerations are continuously examined and addressed.

As emotionally intelligent AI continues to evolve, so too must our ethical frameworks. By prioritizing privacy, consent, and transparency, we can navigate the ethical terrain with a compass guided by the fundamental principles of respect and dignity. This journey is not solely about technological innovation but about ensuring that as we step into the future, we do so with a commitment to ethical stewardship that honors the depth and complexity of human emotion.

## Case Studies: Emotional Intelligence in AI Applications

Diving into the realm of real-world applications, we uncover intriguing instances where emotional intelligence has been seamlessly integrated into AI systems, demonstrating not just theoretical potential but practical utility. These case studies serve as beacons, guiding the path for future innovations in the field.

One remarkable example is the development of emotionally aware virtual assistants. These sophisticated AI entities are equipped with the ability to detect subtle cues in a user's voice tone, inflection, and even choice of words, enabling them to adapt their responses accordingly. This adaptation might manifest in varied forms, such as offering comforting words during a discernible moment of distress or adopting a more upbeat cadence to match a user's excitement. This level of responsiveness elevates the user experience, making interactions feel less transactional and more genuinely engaging.

Another compelling application is found within the healthcare sector, where AI-driven platforms are being designed to assist in mental health therapy. By analyzing speech patterns and facial expressions, these systems can identify indicators of emotional distress or well-being, offering therapists a nuanced understanding of a patient's emotional state over time. Such insights can enrich therapy sessions, allowing for more targeted and effective interventions.

In the educational sphere, emotionally intelligent AI is transforming how learning is facilitated. Educational software, equipped with emotion recognition capabilities, can adjust the pace of instruction or the complexity of content based on the learner's emotional signals, like confusion or frustration. This personalized approach not only enhances learning outcomes but also fosters a more supportive and encouraging learning environment.

These case studies exemplify the transformative impact emotional intelligence is having across various domains, illustrating a future where AI doesn't just process information but connects, supports, and enhances human experiences in profound ways. Each application showcases the promise of emotional intelligence in AI: to create systems that understand us better and in doing so, enrich our lives in unexpected and meaningful ways.

## The Future of Emotional Intelligence in AI

As we venture further into the integration of emotional intelligence within artificial intelligence, the horizon of possibilities stretches out before us, inviting a revolution in how we engage with machines. This evolution toward emotionally intelligent AI heralds a new era where our digital companions are not just repositories of data but entities that can sense, understand, and react to our emotional states with a finesse that rivals human intuition. The promise of these advancements lies in crafting systems that offer more than mere functionality—they strive to comprehend and participate in the human experience in a way that is both profound and subtle.

Imagine a world where your devices can anticipate your needs not just based on your browsing history or shopping habits, but by genuinely understanding the tone of your day or the mood behind your messages. This future, where technology can empathize and adapt to our emotional ebbs and flows, offers a canvas for innovation that goes beyond convenience, aiming for a connection that enhances our daily lives in meaningful ways.

In pushing the boundaries of what machines can understand about human emotions, we are also redefining the landscape of human-machine interaction. This not only involves sophisticated algorithms and cutting-edge technology but also a deep commitment to ethical considerations, ensuring that these emotionally intelligent systems enhance well-being without compromising our values or autonomy.

As we move toward this emotionally intelligent AI future, the journey will be marked by challenges and opportunities alike. The potential for technology to truly understand and interact with us on an emotional level opens up new avenues for personalization, accessibility, and empathy in our digital world, forging a future where technology supports not just our tasks, but also our humanity.

## Preparing for an Emotionally Intelligent AI World

As we edge closer to a future interwoven with emotionally intelligent AI, the necessity to lay a strong, informed foundation cannot be understated. Navigating this new landscape requires a proactive approach to education, ensuring that both creators and users of AI have a thorough understanding of its emotional capabilities and implications. This education goes beyond mere technical know-how, extending into the ethical realm, where discussions about the moral use of emotional data take center stage.

A critical aspect of this preparation involves setting clear, stringent guidelines for the development of emotionally intelligent AI. These guidelines must underscore the importance of ethical considerations, from the initial design phase through to deployment, ensuring that these systems are developed with a deep respect for privacy, consent, and inclusivity. By embedding these values at the core of AI development, we pave the way for technology that not only understands our emotions but does so with integrity.

Transparency plays a pivotal role in this preparation phase. Both developers and users should engage in an open dialogue about how emotional data is collected, analyzed, and utilized. This transparency is crucial for building trust and ensuring that users feel comfortable and secure in their interactions with emotionally intelligent AI. It also fosters an environment where ethical concerns can be addressed promptly, and adjustments made as needed.

By focusing on education, ethical guidelines, and transparency, we can embrace the advancements of emotionally intelligent AI while safeguarding our fundamental human values. This preparation ensures that as we step into a future enriched by AI, we do so with confidence and a collective commitment to using technology to enhance, not undermine, our human experience.

# CHAPTER 11: THE HIDDEN LINK BETWEEN EMOTIONAL INTELLIGENCE AND NON-DUAL ABUNDANCE

Emotional intelligence is a powerful tool that can lead to personal growth and fulfillment. When combined with the concept of non-dual holistic prosperity, it can unlock a deeper level of abundance and contentment in life. By understanding the link between emotional intelligence and non-dual abundance, individuals can cultivate a more balanced and harmonious existence.

## Unveiling Emotional Intelligence: A Foundation for Personal Growth

Emotional intelligence emerges not just as a skill set but as a core pillar supporting personal development and flourishing. At its heart, it's about harnessing the power of recognizing, understanding, and adeptly managing one's own emotions, alongside the capacity to tune into the emotions of others with sensitivity and acumen. This profound understanding and interaction with emotions fuel not only self-improvement but also empower individuals to steer through the myriad of interpersonal dynamics with grace and effectiveness.

The journey to cultivate emotional intelligence is both introspective and outward-facing. It demands a relentless pursuit of self-awareness, where one continually peels back the layers of their emotional experiences to uncover deeper insights into their own behaviors and triggers. This self-discovery process is instrumental in fostering self-regulation, where the knowledge of one's emotional states becomes the bedrock for exercising control and adaptability in emotional expressions. The ripple effect of this self-mastery is far-reaching, enhancing one's ability to stay motivated, navigate stress, and rebound from setbacks with resilience.

Moreover, the evolution of emotional intelligence is marked by an expanding circle of empathy. The capability to empathize, to genuinely step into the shoes of another, transcends mere emotional acuity; it becomes a bridge to profound human connection. Through empathy, individuals forge stronger, more meaningful relationships, marked by a deep understanding and mutual respect. This shared emotional landscape paves the way for heightened social skills, enabling smoother interactions, conflict resolution, and collaborative success in both personal and professional spheres.

In essence, emotional intelligence is not merely an asset but a necessity for those aiming for personal growth. It is through the nuanced management of emotions and the cultivation of empathy that individuals unlock their potential, fostering a life rich in connections and personal achievement.

## The Spectrum of Non-Dual Holistic Prosperity: Beyond the Material

At the heart of non-dual holistic prosperity lies a profound and expansive understanding of wealth that transcends the traditional metrics of success and accumulation of material assets. This concept of abundance invites us into a world where prosperity is not just quantified by what we possess but by the depth of our inner peace, emotional resilience, and the richness of our connections with others and the environment.

In navigating the terrain of non-dual holistic prosperity, we uncover a dimension of abundance that is inherently inclusive and sustainable, fostering a sense of completeness that isn't shaken by external fluctuations. It encourages a shift from a scarcity mindset, where one is perpetually seeking more, to an awareness of plenitude in the present moment. Here, prosperity is seen as an endless stream of opportunities for growth, learning, and contribution, flowing from a wellspring of internal resources—creativity, compassion, wisdom, and resilience.

The cultivation of such prosperity requires a conscious move away from dualistic thinking, which often pits the self against the other, the spiritual against the material, or the individual against the collective. Instead, it promotes an integrated approach to living, where there is no separation between personal well-being and the well-being of the community and the natural world. This holistic perspective recognizes that true abundance flourishes in the context of interconnectedness and mutual care.

Embracing non-dual holistic prosperity also means acknowledging the intrinsic value of emotional and spiritual wealth. It involves enriching one's life with experiences that nurture the soul, deepen introspection, and enhance one's capacity for empathy and compassion. In this landscape, success is measured by the quality of our relationships, the tranquility of our minds, and our ability to live in harmony with the natural world.

Thus, non-dual holistic prosperity unfolds as a journey towards integrating all aspects of our being, fostering a life that is not only abundant in external achievements but is profoundly fulfilling and meaningful on every level.

## Navigating the Emotional Landscape: The Role of Self-Awareness

Self-awareness stands as a fundamental pillar in the journey toward emotional intelligence, acting as the compass that guides us through the intricate emotional landscape of our lives. It's the first step in recognizing the nuances of our feelings, thoughts, and the motivations behind our actions. With self-awareness, we delve into the depths of our inner world, identifying patterns and triggers that shape our emotional responses. This introspective quest not only illuminates the pathways to personal growth but also equips us with the clarity to make informed decisions, fostering an environment of self-improvement and adaptability.

Cultivating self-awareness is akin to learning a new language—the language of the self. It requires patience, curiosity, and the willingness to confront sometimes uncomfortable truths about our character and behaviors. By engaging in practices such as mindfulness meditation, journaling, or reflective contemplation, we enhance our self-awareness, allowing for a more nuanced understanding of our emotional state. This understanding is crucial for recognizing how our emotions influence our thoughts and actions, and vice versa, creating a feedback loop that either propels us forward or holds us back.

In the grand tapestry of emotional intelligence, self-awareness serves as the thread that connects our inner experiences with the outer world. It empowers us to navigate our emotions with grace, setting the stage for the development of other critical emotional intelligence competencies, such as empathy, emotional regulation, and effective communication. As we become more attuned to the ebbs and flows of our emotional states, we lay the groundwork for meaningful interactions and deeper connections with others, enhancing our capacity for empathy and understanding.

By embracing self-awareness, we open ourselves to the transformative potential of emotional intelligence, embarking on a journey that not only enriches our personal lives but also elevates our interactions with the world around us. It's through this self-discovery process that we can truly begin to craft a life of non-dual holistic prosperity, where emotional wealth and interpersonal harmony coalesce, leading to a more abundant and fulfilled existence.

## Empathy: The Bridge to Connecting and Understanding Others

Empathy stands as a cornerstone within the architecture of emotional intelligence, offering a gateway through which we traverse the landscape of human emotion and connection. It's not merely about the capacity to perceive the emotions of those around us but involves a deeper, more engaged process of feeling with and for others, standing in solidarity with their emotional experiences. This profound engagement fosters a sense of shared humanity, breaking down the barriers that often isolate us in our personal silos of experience.

The cultivation of empathy requires a deliberate practice of putting ourselves in others' shoes, imagining the world from their perspective, and responding with kindness and understanding. It's an active endeavor, a choice to engage with the world in a way that acknowledges the complex tapestry of human emotion and respects the intrinsic value of diverse experiences. By nurturing empathy, we not only enhance our ability to communicate effectively but also enrich our capacity for compassion, forging bonds that are built on genuine understanding and mutual respect.

In the realm of non-dual holistic prosperity, empathy plays an indispensable role. It aligns with the principle that our well-being is inextricably linked with the well-being of others and the world at large. Through empathy, we recognize that true abundance flourishes not in isolation but in the richness of our relationships and the depth of our connections. It prompts us to act with generosity and kindness, contributing to a collective abundance that benefits all.

Empathy, therefore, is not just a bridge to understanding others; it is also a pathway to transforming our interactions and fostering a world where holistic prosperity is shared. As we become more attuned to the emotions of those around us, we are better equipped to navigate the complexities of human relationships, paving the way for a more compassionate, interconnected existence.

## Mastering Emotional Regulation: Strategies for Well-Being

Emotional regulation stands as a linchpin in our quest for mental equilibrium and robust health, offering a pathway to navigate the tempestuous seas of our emotions with dexterity and poise. The mastery of this skill empowers us to face the world with a balanced perspective, ensuring our responses to life's ups and downs are measured and constructive rather than reactive and destabilizing.

Key to achieving this mastery is the cultivation of techniques that anchor us during emotional storms. Practices such as deep breathing serve as a physical bridge, bringing us back to a state of calm and centeredness. The simple act of focusing on the breath can act as a powerful tool to diffuse the intensity of immediate emotional reactions, providing a space for more reflective and considered responses.

Mindfulness meditation further enhances our capacity for emotional regulation. By fostering an attentive and non-judgmental awareness of the present moment, mindfulness allows us to observe our emotions without being swept away by them. This practice not only aids in recognizing our emotional triggers but also in diminishing the power they have over our actions and reactions.

Positive self-talk, another vital strategy, helps to reframe our internal narrative. By challenging and replacing negative thoughts with affirmations of our strength and resilience, we nurture a more supportive and empowering inner dialogue. This shift in perspective is crucial for maintaining emotional stability and fostering a sense of well-being, even in the face of adversity.

Together, these strategies form a toolkit for emotional regulation, essential for navigating the complexities of our inner landscape. As we refine our ability to manage our emotions, we open doors to enhanced personal growth, deeper relational connections, and a more harmonious existence. The journey towards emotional regulation is, indeed, a cornerstone in the edifice of holistic prosperity, laying the groundwork for a life lived with intention, understanding, and grace.

## The Art of Effective Communication: Expressing Needs and Boundaries

Mastering the art of effective communication is akin to navigating a river with both precision and care, ensuring that our words do not erode the banks of our relationships, but rather, enrich the soils on which they stand. Expressing our needs and boundaries is an integral part of this journey, requiring a delicate balance of honesty, respect, and understanding. This dynamic process allows us to articulate our deepest truths and limits in a manner that fosters mutual respect and understanding, rather than discord or resentment.

In the realm of emotional intelligence, effective communication is not merely about the transmission of information; it's an exchange that is imbued with empathy, active listening, and responsiveness. When we express our needs, we do so with a vulnerability that invites connection, and when we set boundaries, we do so with a strength that commands respect.

This duality is essential for maintaining the integrity of our personal space while nurturing the growth of our relationships.

Developing this skill set begins with a profound self-awareness, an understanding of our values, needs, and the non-negotiables in our lives. It is from this foundation of self-knowledge that we can communicate our boundaries clearly and confidently, without fear of overstepping or being misunderstood. Furthermore, by actively listening and responding with empathy to others, we create a reciprocal environment where communication thrives on mutual respect and understanding.

Thus, the art of effective communication is a dynamic interplay of expressing and listening, giving and receiving. It is a testament to the depth of our emotional intelligence, enabling us to navigate the complexities of human relationships with grace and efficacy. Through this lens, we see that expressing our needs and boundaries is not a barrier to connection, but a bridge to deeper, more meaningful interactions.

## The Power of Emotional Intelligence in Leadership

In the realm of leadership, emotional intelligence emerges as a transformative force, casting a long shadow over traditional notions of what it means to lead. At the core of effective leadership lies the ability to navigate the complex web of human emotions with finesse and insight. Leaders vested with a high degree of emotional intelligence possess an unparalleled advantage – the capacity to resonate with, inspire, and mobilize their teams toward shared goals and visions.

The essence of leadership infused with emotional intelligence is not about command and control but about fostering an environment of trust, respect, and mutual understanding. Such leaders are adept at reading the room, discerning unspoken concerns, and addressing them in a manner that uplifts and motivates. They recognize that the heart of true leadership is the power of connection – connecting with individuals on a level that transcends mere professional interaction and touches upon their intrinsic motivations, fears, and aspirations.

Moreover, emotionally intelligent leaders are masters of adaptability. They possess the unique ability to modulate their leadership style to meet the diverse needs of their team members. Whether it's through providing support and encouragement, offering constructive feedback, or challenging their team to exceed their own expectations, these leaders know how to bring out the best in people.

Their approach to conflict resolution further exemplifies their emotional acumen. Instead of allowing conflicts to escalate or simmer, they address them head-on, with a focus on understanding and reconciliation. By doing so, they not only resolve immediate issues but also build a foundation of stronger, more resilient relationships.

In essence, the infusion of emotional intelligence into leadership transforms the very fabric of organizational dynamics. It shifts the paradigm from mere productivity and efficiency to one of growth, fulfillment, and collective achievement. Such leadership not only elevates individuals but also propels the organization toward a future marked by innovation, cohesion, and holistic prosperity.

## Integrating Emotional Intelligence into

## Daily Life for Holistic Prosperity

Embodying emotional intelligence in our everyday lives is akin to cultivating a garden of holistic prosperity, where the seeds of self-awareness, empathy, emotional regulation, and effective communication are nurtured into flourishing blooms. This garden does not thrive overnight; it requires daily attention, care, and a commitment to growth. Each day presents a new canvas on which to practice the art of emotional intelligence, be it through mindful interactions with others, introspective moments of self-reflection, or in the quiet solitude where we learn to regulate our deepest emotions.

To weave emotional intelligence into the fabric of our daily existence, we start by setting intentions. These intentions act as guiding stars, illuminating the path toward more conscious and intentional living. They remind us to pause, to breathe, and to choose responses rather than react impulsively. In the complexity of our interactions, we strive to listen actively, to empathize deeply, and to communicate with clarity and compassion. These are not merely acts of self-improvement but gestures of profound respect for the shared human experience.

In the mundane moments, the practice of emotional intelligence might manifest as a silent acknowledgment of our emotional state or a gentle reminder to ourselves that growth is a process, not a destination. It is in the challenges that this practice reveals its true power, transforming obstacles into opportunities for learning and connection.

Embracing emotional intelligence daily empowers us to navigate life's highs and lows with grace, to foster relationships that are rooted in mutual understanding, and to contribute to a world that values holistic prosperity. Through this daily integration, we not only enhance our personal well-being but also become catalysts for positive change in the lives of those around us, embodying the essence of non-dual abundance.

## Overcoming Barriers to Emotional Intelligence

Navigating the path to heightened emotional intelligence is akin to embarking on a deep-sea voyage; the journey is fraught with challenges that test the resilience of our emotional vessel. Central among these challenges are internal barriers such as entrenched fear, persistent self-doubt, corrosive negative self-talk, and the heavy shadows cast by past experiences. These obstacles, if left unaddressed, can anchor us away from the shores of emotional growth and hinder our journey toward holistic prosperity.

To set sail beyond these barriers, a conscious and deliberate effort is required. It starts with the recognition and acknowledgment of these impediments, shining a light on them rather than allowing them to lurk beneath the surface. Addressing fear demands courage to confront what makes us vulnerable, understanding that true emotional strength is born from vulnerability. Overcoming self-doubt requires the cultivation of self-compassion, affirming that we are enough as we are and that growth is a continuous process. To silence negative self-talk, we must become vigilant guardians of our inner dialogue, challenging and replacing harmful narratives with empowering affirmations.

Moreover, the shadows of past experiences can cloud our emotional landscape, making it imperative to engage in reflective practices that allow for healing and reconciliation with our histories. Through mindfulness, therapy, or supportive dialogues, we can unpack these experiences, learn from them, and ultimately, release their hold on our emotional well-being.

Each step taken to overcome these barriers is a stride toward mastering the art of emotional intelligence, enabling us to navigate life's tumultuous waters with greater ease and resilience, and moving us closer to a state of non-dual abundance.

# THE FUTURE OF EMOTIONAL INTELLIGENCE AND NON-DUAL PROSPERITY

As we look toward the horizon, the symbiosis between emotional intelligence and non-dual holistic prosperity becomes increasingly pivotal. This evolving landscape suggests a promising paradigm where the cultivation of emotional intelligence is not just a personal endeavor but a collective journey toward universal abundance. In this future, the principles of emotional intelligence—self-awareness, empathy, emotional regulation, and effective communication—serve as cornerstones for societal progress, fostering environments where individuals not only thrive independently but also uplift those around them.

The integration of these concepts heralds a shift from traditional success metrics to a broader, more inclusive definition of prosperity—one that values emotional and spiritual fulfillment equally with material achievement. This new era invites us to imagine a world where our interactions are guided by empathy and understanding, and where our collective well-being is prioritized.

In embracing this future, we unlock the full potential of non-dual holistic prosperity, charting a course toward a society where emotional intelligence is at the heart of our shared journey toward abundance. As we move forward, the union of emotional intelligence and non-dual prosperity offers a beacon of hope—a promise of a more connected, compassionate, and abundant world for all.

# ACKNOWLEDGMENTS

First and foremost, I want to express my deepest gratitude to my mother. Your heartfelt support has been the cornerstone of my journey. Your unwavering belief in me has been a constant source of strength and inspiration. Thank you for always being my guiding light.

To Andrew, thank you for always being there. Your steadfast presence and encouragement have been invaluable. Whether in moments of doubt or celebration, you have been a rock of support, and I am profoundly grateful for your friendship and loyalty.

Amy, you are the type of person who makes the world a better place just by existing. Your kindness, positivity, and genuine spirit have been a beacon of hope and joy. Thank you for being a source of light and for reminding me of the goodness in the world.

Lastly, to Laurie, your unconditional support has been a lifeline. Your unwavering faith in me and your constant encouragement have made all the difference. Thank you for standing by me through every challenge and triumph. Your support has been a gift beyond measure.

I also want to extend my gratitude to whatever creative force there is in the universe for bringing me back to life, moving through me to create Luminous Prosperity, dozens of books, classes, and the purpose of serving the world by changing the way we relate to wealth. Thank you for guiding me on this incredible journey.

# ABOUT THE AUTHOR

Ammanuel Santa Anna is a distinguished life and executive coach, dedicated to helping individuals unlock their full potential and achieve holistic prosperity. As the founder of Luminous Prosperity, Ammanuel has guided countless clients through transformative journeys, empowering them to master their emotions, reduce stress, and develop emotional intelligence in all areas of life—from work to play.

With a deep understanding of emotional intelligence, Ammanuel combines his expertise as a life coach and empath to offer personalized coaching that addresses the unique needs of each client. His approach is rooted in empathy, self-awareness, and a profound commitment to personal growth, making him a sought-after coach for those looking to enhance their emotional intelligence and achieve lasting success.

Beyond his professional endeavors, Ammanuel is a passionate artist and musician. He finds joy in playing several different instruments and expressing himself through poetry, painting, and dance. His love for shellfish and the arts reflects his belief in the importance of a balanced and fulfilling life.

Ammanuel's holistic approach to coaching not only focuses on professional achievements but also on personal well-being and creative expression. His clients appreciate his genuine care, insightful guidance, and the transformative impact of his coaching.

Visit **Luminous Prosperity** to learn more about Ammanuel Santa Anna's coaching services and embark on your journey towards emotional intelligence and holistic prosperity. Whether you're seeking to excel in your career, improve your relationships, or find inner peace, Ammanuel is here to guide you every step of the way.

# RECOMMENDED READING BY AMMANUEL SANTA ANNA

If you enjoyed "The Luminous Prosperity Guide to Emotional Intelligence," you might also find these books by Ammanuel Santa Anna insightful and transformative. Each book delves into different aspects of emotional intelligence, holistic living, and personal growth, offering practical advice and profound insights to help you thrive in all areas of your life.

# 1. THE PLAYFUL PATH: OVERCOMING RSD WITH JOY AND CONFIDENCE

# FORMAT: PAPERBACK, KINDLE

Description: Embark on a transformative journey with "The Playful Path: Navigating Rejection Sensitive Dysphoria with Humor and Joy." This groundbreaking book is tailored for individuals grappling with the intense emotional landscape of Rejection Sensitive Dysphoria (RSD). Ammanuel Santa Anna provides readers with a unique perspective on turning sensitivity into strength and vulnerability into victory. Through heartfelt reflections and laughter-filled exercises, this book encourages readers to find joy in their daily lives and view their sensitivity as a strength, not a setback.

Link: **The Playful Path: Overcoming RSD With Joy and Confidence**

# 2. THE ALCHEMY OF PROSPERITY: UNVEILING YOUR INNER RENAISSANCE THROUGH SPIRITUAL WEALTH

# FORMAT: PAPERBACK, KINDLE

Description: Discover a transformative approach to prosperity with "The Alchemy of Prosperity: Unveiling Your Inner Renaissance Through Spiritual Wealth." This book challenges the conventional notion of wealth, inviting you to explore a holistic perspective that goes beyond material possessions. Ammanuel Santa Anna guides you on a journey towards spiritual wealth, teaching you to transmute external wealth into internal riches through the alchemical process of prosperity. Learn to align your financial goals with your deepest spiritual values, creating a life of purpose and meaning.

Link: **The Alchemy of Prosperity: Unveiling Your Inner Renaissance Through Spiritual Wealth**

# 3. THE SPIRITUAL EXECUTIVE: HOW TO THRIVE IN EVERY AREA OF LIFE

# FORMAT: PAPERBACK, KINDLE

Description: In "The Spiritual Executive," Ammanuel Santa Anna shares his profound insights and transformational strategies that have empowered executives to thrive in every area of their lives. This book unveils the secrets to integrating spirituality seamlessly into the corporate world, helping you lead with authenticity, purpose, and unwavering ethics. Learn how to balance your professional and personal life, achieving a sense of fulfillment and tranquility that extends beyond the boardroom.

Link: **The Spiritual Executive: How to Thrive In Every Area of Life**

# 4. TWIN FLAMES: THE ULTIMATE GUIDE